*THE*

# Benicia State Capitol

JAMES E. LESSENGER | *Featuring Photography by Reg Page*

THE
History
PRESS

Published by The History Press
Charleston, SC
www.historypress.com

Copyright © 2019 by James E. Lessenger
All rights reserved

First published 2019

Manufactured in the United States

ISBN 9781467143844

Library of Congress Control Number: 2019945070

*For Quinn and Eve*

# Contents

# Acknowledgements

The brick, stone and wood Greek Revival Benicia state capitol building stands at the corner of First and H Streets and has survived political struggles, wars and natural disasters for more than 150 years. The story of the building and its changing functions starts before the gold rush, with Rancho Suscol and Robert Semple's arrival in California. It is a story of the founding of the State of California, the people who created it and the intense national and regional politics that shaped it. It is also the story of bribes, duels and successes, as well as some corruption and a bright future.

I have relied heavily on a doctoral dissertation by Sister Mary Grace Kos, CSC, BS, and a master's thesis by David D. Clinton. These two documents were intensely researched, authoritative and well written. Two research tools that have made their appearances in the last ten years and were extremely helpful are the California Digital Newspaper Collection and the Digital Archives of the California State Legislature. The legislature now has its journals online, and they were especially helpful in reporting on the period when the state capitol was in Benicia.

The Benicia Historical Museum was essential in providing research and archive materials. The Steve DeBenedetti collection was important for its completeness and accuracy. The museum's digital collection provided many of the photographs used in this book. I am grateful to my friends and colleagues at the museum for their help and assistance—especially board member and photographer Reg Page, curator Beverly Phelan, archivist Bob Kwasnicka, board president Bob Rozett and executive director Elizabeth d'Huart.

I am also grateful for help from Karen Burns, Carol Berman and Mike Caplin of the Benicia State Parks Association, who provided me with tours, interviews and documents. The California State Library, the State Lands Commission and the California Department of Parks and Recreation were also helpful in providing access to archival materials. Lorie Tinfow, Benicia city manager and fellow Rotarian, was instrumental in allowing me access to the city archives, which is located in a dusty dungeon under the current city hall.

Most importantly, I am appreciative of my wife, Leslie H. Lessenger, PhD, for emotional and editorial support.

This history starts with the land on which the Benicia state capitol stood and who owned that land. Or, more precisely, who had claim to it. The battle over land and the cloud over the title to the entire city of Benicia overshadowed California politics while the legislature met in Benicia during the mid-nineteenth century. Land ownership was the "mother's milk" of California politics at the time and drove all other political debates and issues. The question of land ownership was fought by hired guns in the countryside, diplomats in the negotiating rooms and lawyers in the courts. It reached Congress, the presidency and, finally, the U.S. Supreme Court.

But first, there was inauguration day.

JAMES E. LESSENGER, AB, MD
Benicia, California, 2018

# Benicia

## Inauguration Day

Reverend Sylvester Woodbridge walked up the steps of the new capitol building and scraped the mud off his boots on the iron mud scraper. The weather was cold and windy, as usual for that time of year, and a fine drizzle had just stopped. He had been chosen to give the benedictions at the start of meetings of the legislature in Benicia, but this day was special. The third governor of the new state of California was due to be re-inaugurated. There was some confusion among the crowd that Woodbridge passed as he entered the cramped foyer. Was this the fifth year of statehood or the fourth? Also, who really owned the land on which the building and the city stood? Was General Vallejo the owner, or was his claim invalid as many people claimed?[1]

These were questions for a later time. The building smelled of freshly cut lumber, new furniture and wet paint. There was also the pervasive perfume of cow and pig dung from the innumerable animals that roamed the streets of Benicia and the rest of California. That was another problem for the legislature to—literally—clean up. Roving pigs had become a problem as big as the need for prisons and schools. Several wagon accidents had occurred in San Francisco as pigs ran between the legs of horses and tripped them.

Woodbridge walked past the four anterooms. They were the offices of the clerks who recorded everything that went on in the government, including the legislature. The state was already deeply in debt, but you wouldn't know that from all the smiling faces and backslapping.

*Right*: Reverend Sylvester Woodbridge, circa 1860. *Courtesy Benicia Historical Museum*.

*Below*: The Benicia State Capitol building as seen in 2019. *Courtesy Reg Page*.

The restored assembly chambers as they looked in 2018. *Courtesy Reg Page.*

There were a lot of items on the shopping lists of the state senators and representatives as Woodbridge walked through the inner doors and into the warmth of the downstairs meeting room. The new state had to create— out of whole cloth—a system of education for children. It needed to create colleges and universities. It needed roads, prisons and a militia to protect the citizenry from bandits.

Always in demand for his baritone speaking voice and eloquent words, Woodbridge greeted the members of the legislature who were warming themselves by the wood stove and discussing the major issues of the day. The subject of the Indians came up. The fate of the Indians made Woodbridge wince. He had written to President Zachary Taylor about the need to set aside large swaths of land for the Indians and to protect them from the hired guns who were killing them in droves. Nevertheless, the carnage continued.

The members were unhappy. Benicia had a shortage of lodgings and restaurants, although it did have a few good taverns where the locally brewed German beer flowed liberally. There was also the problem of transportation, with only two mud-sodden routes into the city by land and one route by water. Sacramento, the top contender for the capital, had three routes by water and seven by land. It also had a lot of good hotels and, most importantly, plenty of taverns. Sacramento was also home to lots of wealthy business owners who could come up with the kind of money needed to bribe and buy their way to making their town the capital.

The senate organized itself, and Woodbridge said the prayer as he had every day since the beginning of the stay of the state government in Benicia the previous year. When he finished, the senate got to work, and he walked upstairs to say a prayer for the assembly.

In the foyer again, Woodbridge shook hands with David Broderick, the subject of the Peck Affair and a staunch Free-Soiler. Free-Soilers and abolitionists were putting on a lot of pressure on the State of California to completely eliminate slavery. Woodbridge's own church, Presbyterian, was splintering. A large abolitionist contingent sided with the Congregationalists and the Methodists. The smaller part of the church, the Southern congregations, were digging in and siding with the slavers and secessionists. California had come into the Union as a free state and had prohibited slavery in its constitution, but that didn't matter. Slavery was the law of the land in the United States—even in California. The Full Faith and Credit clause of the Constitution assured that. Slaves were working in the livery stable around the corner from the new capitol and in the mines of the Mother Lode.

Many of the men in the room, including Governor Bigler, resented the slaves in California. There were those who had moral objections and others who had legal objections to slaves in a so-called free state. Most of the men also objected to the fact that Southern slavers were bringing slaves in coffles to work the mines, thus providing competition for free or white miners. Woodbridge knew all of the arguments.

Shaking hands and waving, Woodbridge worked the crowd in the foyer and on the steps, as he was always known to do. Like others in the room, he owned property in town and ran cattle on the range east of Benicia. He was deeply concerned with the question of who owned the land that had once been Rancho Suscol. The old Mexican mission rancho was where Benicia and the new state capital were located. Fierce lawsuits were winding their way through the federal courts over whether General Vallejo actually owned the land he sold to Robert Semple to build Benicia.

Land and water were the "mother's milk" of California politics. The legislature had passed more than a dozen statutes the previous year in Benicia concerning public works, water allocations and land ownership. More statutes were proposed, including several by legislators who thought that women could own land separate from their husbands. Imagine that.

Speaking of women, Woodbridge and Benicia had a better track record of gender equality than most other areas of the state. Woodbridge had started the first women's school in California, the Benicia Young Ladies Seminary, where his own daughter was being educated. And, after all, the village was named after a woman—Francesca Maria Felipa Benicia Carrillo de Vallejo, General Vallejo's wife.

Reporters from Sacramento, San Francisco, San Jose and other parts of the state, including Benicia, circled the building like vultures searching for a dead cow. With some luck, they'd find a juicy scandal. They'd found one in the Peck Affair and in the battle over slavery between David C. Broderick, a Free-Soiler who despised slavery, and David S. Terry, the state supreme court chief justice and an unrepentant slaver.

The conversation around the woodstove, in the taverns and on the streets always came back to the budget. With a state to build, the legislature had spent—some said wasted—thousands of dollars dragging the capital around the state. First San Jose, then Vallejo, then Sacramento, then Vallejo and now Benicia. It was no secret that many of the people in Benicia that day, including Governor Bigler, preferred Sacramento. San Jose was out, primarily because of Cayote Creek, which turned the city into a sea of mud every spring. The Vallejo experience had been a fraud in every sense of the word. The general had promised an intact capital with buildings, streets, hotels and the all-important taverns. All that awaited the legislature when they arrived was a vermin-infested shack. Within days, the state government left for Benicia.

Adding to the budget woes of Woodbridge and the rest of the men lining up to watch the military procession up First Street with the new governor in tow were the California Rangers. A tremendous amount of money was being spent by the state to chase down the bandits who roamed the countryside of California. If they only robbed stage lines and banks, it wouldn't be so emotional to those meeting in Benicia that day. But there were reports circulating Benicia of bandits raiding farms, then assaulting and killing the inhabitants.

Woodbridge took a quick tour of the capitol. He had watched it being built and shared civic pride with the rest of the inhabitants of Benicia. The entry foyer led to a hallway with four rooms on each side for the offices of the state. Double doors led to the senate chamber and its rows of desks—one for each senator. A raised dais where the officers could preside was at the end of the room.

Walking up the narrow spiral stairs, the lanky Woodbridge made it to the upper floor. Only two rooms flanked the hall that led to the assembly chambers, which was laid out in the same manner as the senate chamber downstairs.

A letter press used for copying documents. *Courtesy Reg Page.*

One of two stairs to the upper floor. *Courtesy Reg Page.*

That was all there was to the building. Simple and straight forward—even Puritan—it was Puritan Greek temple. There was something incongruous about the sight of a Greek temple jutting up from a California frontier town. The problem was, everyone knew that the building was already too small for a state that was the second largest in the Union. But it was time for the inauguration.

Under the command of Captain Gorman, the San Francisco Blues mustered to attention in front of the St. Charles Hotel, which was one of the hastily constructed buildings at the foot of First Street near the city wharf. A Mr. Coffroth, as chairman of the inauguration committee, addressed Captain Gorham and invited the company to participate in the proceedings of the inauguration. John Bigler, already the governor for two years, exited the hotel and followed a procession led by the Union Band, also of San Francisco. People from all over the state had come to watch the inauguration, and they cheered as the procession made its way uphill to the capitol, ignoring the rivulets of water washing down the dirt road. Many citizens joined the procession.

The assembly chambers. The table in the foreground is probably from the original capitol, and the remaining are reproductions. *Courtesy Reg Page.*

Portrait of Governor John Bigler that now hangs in the Old State Capitol State Park in Benicia. *Courtesy Reg Page.*

Woodbridge sized up Bigler, a man he had met many times. A gruff Northern Yankee, Honest John, as he was known, was a Mormon. He was one of those people who got down to work with a minimum of fuss and feathers. He also didn't smoke or drink, which made him stick out in California.

At the capitol, the sergeant-at-arms announced, "His excellency the governor," who then entered the hall and appeared in excellent health and spirits. He was escorted by the inauguration committee to a seat beside the president of the senate. The entire first floor of the building was crammed with members of the guard, the band, wives of dignitaries and people of all stripes. Reporters crowded to the front with notebooks in hand. A thick fog of cigar smoke flooded the room, and the faint odor of the privy—outside the west-facing windows—floated in.

The oath of office was administered to the governor by Judge Winston of Solano County, after which Bigler delivered his inaugural address to a silent crowd. With so many issues facing the state, Bigler could have spoken forever. But to the relief of Woodbridge, and no doubt the rest of the audience, the speech was short. His speech was optimistic and laid out a bright future for the state. Following the inauguration, as was befitting a legislature of a thousand drinks, the party retreated to the nearby saloons to celebrate.

Woodbridge walked down the street to his home. Benicia was the place to be. But there was the problem with the title of the land. It hovered over Benicia like an axe ready to fall.

# Rancho Suscol

## Land Issues in California

L
and was the base issue of politics in California during the time the capitol was in Benicia. The very lot where the building stood was contested and provides an example of land politics across the state. Rancho Suscol encompassed about eighty thousand acres that included what is now Benicia, Vallejo, American Canyon and the western part of the Suisun Marsh in western Solano and southern Napa Counties. The story of the *rancho* starts with the Patwin people and progresses to federal patents on the land. It involves squatters, regulators, the Treaty of Guadalupe Hidalgo, honest and not-so-honest lawyers and men and women of courage and foresight.

### THE PATWIN AND WINTUN PEOPLES

The Patwin and Wintun peoples occupied the area that became the rancho. In the Patwin language, *suscol* means "wet and green" and refers to the marsh lands. The word for "person" in the language of the Patwin people is *patwin*, just as *wintun* and *wintu* are "person" in the Wintun language. The Patwin lived in small bands with fewer than one hundred people and spoke a dialect of the Wintun people, who lived in the Benicia-Vallejo area, the Napa Valley and the Sacramento River Valley. The Patwin were primarily hunter-gathers. They ground acorns

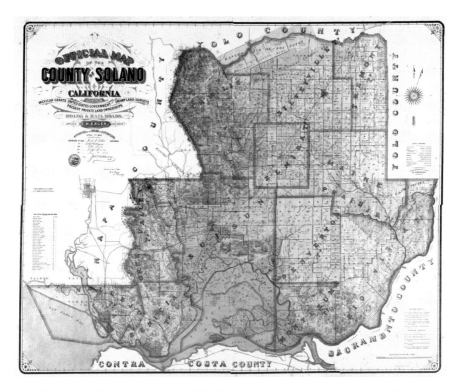

An official map of Solano County in 1890. The rancho also encompassed part of southern Napa County. *Courtesy Benicia Historical Museum.*

on stone implements and traded with tribes to the east for obsidian to made arrowheads. The arrowheads, stone implements and a few baskets are all that remain of their community.[2]

While there may have been limited European contact before 1810, in that year, Captain Gabriel Moraga, the first European born in California, became the first Spaniard to explore the Carquinez Straits. He engaged a large group of Patwin on the shores of the Suisun Marsh, northeast of where the Arsenal resided, and in the ensuing battle, most of the Patwin adults were killed. The surviving children were taken into slavery at Mission Dolores in Yerba Buena, which is now San Francisco. Two decades later, epidemics of smallpox swept through the California Indian tribes. Guadalupe Mariano Vallejo later said that in 1837 there were about forty thousand Indians in the area, and after another epidemic, there were only about two hundred Indians remaining. Today, a small number of people are descended from the Patwin people.[3]

The Patwin, like other Native American tribes, had no concept of land ownership. They migrated along the north shores of the Carquinez Straits based on the weather, availability of food and traditions. A peaceful people, they established their settlements in carefully selected sites to provide water, food and protection according to the seasons. Boundaries such as the ones that exist today were foreign to them.

## Mission San Francisco Solano

Mission San Francisco Solano in Sonoma is located at the northernmost end of the El Camino Real and Mission Road and was the last mission to be founded in California. In 1819, Father José Altamira, a Franciscan trained in Spain, was assigned to Mission Dolores in Yerba Buena. He soon became dissatisfied with the unexciting rhythm of mission life and dreamed a plan to establish a new mission north of Mission San Rafael. Bypassing the church leadership, he applied directly to Governor Luis Argüello for permission to establish the mission. Argüello presented the plan to the Territorial Assembly in Monterey in 1823, and it approved the plan. For good measure, it added the transfer of Mission San Rafael to the new mission. When the ecclesiastical authorities caught word of the plan, they were reportedly enraged at Altamira's insubordination. Three-sided negotiations ensued

Postcard image of Mission San Francisco Solano in Sonoma, California, circa 1860. *Courtesy Benicia Historical Museum.*

between Argüello, Altamira and the bishop in Monterey. These negotiations resulted in the founding of Mission San Francisco Solano, named after St. Francis of Solano, a martyred Peruvian missionary.[4]

The territory that belonged to the mission was enormous and included most of the land north of the Carquinez Straits. Several ranchos, including Petaluma and Suscol, were formed by the mission priests to provide food and income. Unfortunately, Father Altamira relied on flogging and imprisonment to bring the Patwin and Wintun people into the Church, and many fled. Finally, in 1826 the Native Americans rebelled and burned the buildings, forcing Altamira to flee to Mission San Rafael and eventually to Spain. The mission was rebuilt and went through a succession of priests until it was secularized.[5]

## Secularization (Nationalization) into Rancho Nacional Solano

The missions and the Mexican government owned most of the property in California prior to 1830. At that time, only twenty-one pieces of property were in private hands in all of Alta California. Thus there was less property for new immigrants, the sons of the *Californio* Dons and, most importantly, the legions of unemployed Spanish army veterans left to their own devices after Mexico renounced the Spanish Crown in 1821. Further, the Council of the Indies, which ran affairs in the New World for the Spanish Crown, never intended for the missions to be permanent. They were only intended to exist for about ten years while enough neophytes were converted and a pueblo could be established. At that time, the mission churches would become parish churches.[6]

Beginning in 1833, and over the next sixteen years, the missions were secularized by the California department of the Mexican government. The initial plan was to separate the public from the religious segments of the missions and turn the public parts over to the Indians or make them national ranchos for cattle grazing. The missions would then become parish churches. Unaware of the value of their land and inexperienced in matters of land ownership, the Indians quickly lost their land to gamblers and land speculators. Mission Solano was secularized in 1834 and Rancho Nacional Suscol was established, leaving a power vacuum in the northern tier of Mexican California and vast stretches of land to be divided. Stepping into the power void was Guadalupe Mariano Vallejo.[7]

## VALLEJO COMES TO RANCHO NACIONAL SUSCOL

Guadalupe Mariano Vallejo was born at the most distant outpost of the Spanish empire, which lasted from the first voyage of Columbus to the Spanish-American War. Above all else, he was a *Californio*—a Spanish Creole born in California, an officer, a gentleman and an *hombre de razon* (a man of reason and learning). The third son of a Spaniard, Sergeant Ignacio Ferrer Vallejo, and a *Californio*, Maria Antonia Lugo, Vallejo was born into the military at the *presidio* of Monterey on July 4, 1807. In his adolescence, Vallejo attracted the attention of Governor Pablo Vicente de Sola, who became his mentor and taught him that diplomacy could be far more effective than the sword. When Sola returned to Mexico to become part of the first Mexican legislature, Vallejo was appointed to be the personal secretary to Governor Luis Argüello. As semiautonomous state of Mexico, California thrived on the relaxation of the laws, especially those that pertained to the establishment of ranchos.[8]

In 1824, at the age of nineteen, Vallejo became a member of *el diputacion,* the California territorial legislature meeting in Monterey. At the age of twenty-two, he was appointed second lieutenant, and in 1829 he defeated Chief Estanislao and the Miwok Indians, among reports of brutality on both sides. Vallejo next came to the attention of Governor José Figueroa, a prime mover in California history and a man who was part Aztec. In 1832, Vallejo married Francesca Maria Felipa Benicia Carrillo, a member of a wealthy and politically powerful *Californio* family. Vallejo was transferred to the San Francisco presidio, and a year later their first child arrived.[9]

Later that year, Figueroa advanced Vallejo to the rank of general and placed him in command of a military post in Sonoma, adjacent to Mission Solano, and after secularization of the missions, the sixty-six-thousand-acre Rancho Petaluma. During the subsequent decade, General Vallejo made peace with his neighbors—the Russians at Fort Ross, the *padres* of the mission and the remaining Patwin peoples—through a cunning alliance with a seven-foot-tall Patwin he named Chief Solano. Vallejo's large adobe homes on the Sonoma Plaza and at Rancho Petaluma soon became renowned for open hospitality.[10]

In August 1842, General Manuel Micheltorena landed in California with a military force from Mexico City. He was prepared to become the governor of Alta California. Within a year, Micheltorena and his government needed money to create a standing army to deal with

Guadalupe Mariano Vallejo, circa 1860. *Courtesy Benicia Historical Museum.*

increasing American immigration across the Sierra Nevada Mountains. He approached the *Californios* for money, and Vallejo ran a hard bargain. In exchange for five thousand Spanish silver dollars to support a military battalion, Vallejo received eleven thousand Spanish dollars of agricultural equipment and the eighty-thousand-acre Rancho Suscol.[11]

Judge John Currey represented both land owners—called settlers—and the newcomers to the same land—called squatters—in the rancho legal battles that were to follow the American conquest. Curry said about Vallejo,

> *The colonization laws of Mexico did not allow a grant of its public domain of more than 11 Mexican leagues. General Mariano G. Vallejo, the commander-in-chief of all the California military forces north of the Bay of San Francisco and west of the Sacramento River, had been granted the full measure of 11 leagues. He wanted more and coveted the Suscol bounded on the westerly side by the ranch of Cayetano Juarez, near the present city of Napa, and on the south easterly by the Straits of Carquinez, and on the northerly side by the Suisun Bay and swamplands as far as Cordelia or Bridgeport, and thence north westerly of Green Valley to the Twin Peaks in that direction where it reaches the line first mentioned above.*[12]

General Vallejo  received the property, now named Rancho Suscol Nacional, by two means: (1) a colonization grant from the Mexican government on March 15, 1843, and (2) a purchase contract from the Mexican government on June 19, 1844.[13]

Was the transfer of power a sale or an actual land grant? Was the sale legal under Mexican law? Those questions would eventually go to the U.S. Supreme Court.

## A Short Primer on Land Grants

There was a considerable difference between how land grants were issued in the Spanish and Mexican periods of California history. In the Spanish era, the land belonged to the king of Spain and was administered by the viceroy in Mexico City and the governor in Monterey, Alta California. During the Spanish era, the term "land grant" was a misnomer. The king of Spain maintained ownership over all the land, but *concesiones* (concessions) and *reconacimientos* (recognitions) were officially granted to the missions and individual users. Presidios were formed and *ranchos del Rey* (royal ranchos) organized to supply the presidios with food. As the missions were formed, gigantic swaths of land were transferred to the church by concession. These lands were subsequently broken into administrative units of mission ranchos, such as Ranchos Suscol and Petaluma. Military veterans, such as Sergeant José Ortega who discovered San Francisco Harbor, were awarded concessions for large swaths of land distant from the royal and mission ranchos. Lastly, four square leagues were set aside for the use of *pueblos*, where small stores and manufacturing shops were situated and *rancherias* were set aside for the Indian tribes. The Spanish Crown also issued vague cattle grazing permits.[14]

Mexico gained independence in 1821 and organized itself constitutionally in 1824. The Mexican laws of 1824 and 1828 clarified the issues of land ownership so that actual grants of full title could be made. Governors were given authority to grant vacant lands to *empresarios* (contractors), families and Mexican or foreign private citizens who claimed them for cultivation and habitation.[15]

The steps to ownership began with a petition to the governor that contained a written description of the land and a *diseño* or map. Grants made to families and private people were not considered valid without the previous consent of the Territorial Deputation or of the supreme government in Mexico City. Grants to empresarios for colonization purposes required final approval of the supreme government. The laws required the governor to issue a document signed by him "to serve as a title to the person interested" and to keep a record of petitions and grants with the maps of the lands granted. Failure to cultivate or occupy the land within a certain time would void the grant. The colonist was expected to prove cultivation or occupancy before the municipal authority to secure the right of ownership and to freely dispose of the land. In this way, not only were the Petaluma and Suscol Ranchos granted to Mariano Vallejo but Rancho Suisun was also granted to Vallejo's designated substitute, Francisco Solano, "chief of the tribes of the frontiers of Sonoma."[16]

In addition to the ranchos at Suscol and Petaluma, Vallejo owned land in the San Ramon Valley and on the coast. The land owned by Francisco Solano was a front for Vallejo's ownership. By the fourth decade of the nineteenth century, Francisco Solano had become a vassal of Vallejo, who had his own private army of Indians to keep other Indian groups in line, to ward off Mexican and American squatters and to chase off the ever-present *bandidos*. By 1846, the Americans had started to trickle over the Sierra Nevada Mountains and into John Sutter's fort. Vallejo would become the focus of a rebellion and, in the process, would meet Robert Semple.[17]

## Robert Baylor Semple Appears on Rancho Suscol

Dr. Robert Baylor Semple was California's first newspaper reporter, publisher and editor. His newspaper, the *Californian*, was the first newspaper published in California. He was a dentist and had also worked as an attorney, medical doctor, farmer and businessman before traveling west on a wagon train in 1845. He participated in the Bear Flag Revolt of June 10, 1846, when a group of Americans secretly entered Sonoma, captured General Vallejo, manufactured a series of flags with bears on them, raised one of them and then transported Vallejo to Sutter's fort. The United States had declared war on Mexico on May 13, 1846, but the Bear Flaggers didn't know that. Semple assumed the role of the adult of the Bear Flagger raiding party and tempered the hotheads—*los osos* (the bears)—who wanted to shoot up the town and hang people. He and Vallejo

Robert Baylor Semple, circa 1850. *Courtesy Benicia Historical Museum.*

became friends during the ordeal, and Vallejo would later refer to Semple as *el Buen Oso* (the Good Bear). It was Semple who assisted the ailing Vallejo back to Sonoma when he was released. By the time Vallejo returned to Sonoma, the Mexican War was over, and California was part of the United States and was governed by a series of military governors.[18]

Semple was searching for business and land deals and saw the property that is now Benicia on one of his later trips between San Francisco and Sacramento. He first approached the Martinez family with the idea of building a town on the south side of the Carquinez Straits, but opposition from John Walsh and John Frisbie, owners of the land to the east of Martinez, squashed the deal. Semple then approached Vallejo to buy the land that is now Benicia. In the intervening years, Chief Solano died and Vallejo assumed ownership of the rancho. There is no record of what went on in the negotiations between these two hard-crusted businessmen, but Vallejo sold the land (no money changed hands) to Semple for $500 in U.S. gold coins; a promise to name the town after his wife, Francesca; ferry service across the Carquinez Straits; and a school open to all to be financed from the profits of the ferry. In a seemingly petty maneuver, when the *alcalde* of Yerba Buena received word that Semple planned to name his new town Francesca, he immediately changed the name of his small *pueblo* to San Francisco. Semple was left to name his new town Benicia.[19]

The *Californian* printed on December 22, 1846, outlined the contents of the agreement between Vallejo and Semple and started the process of subdividing Rancho Suscol. The nine-part agreement secured for Vallejo an important ferry across the Carquinez Straits to his other future subdivisions.[20]

## ROBERT SEMPLE, LAND DEVELOPER

Semple had no money of his own, so he partnered with Thomas Larkin, the richest man in California at the time, and Bethuel Phelps, a real estate investor. Larkin, former United States counsel to Mexican California, had extensive land holdings and business connections. In 1847, Semple ordered a survey of his future city to be done by Jasper O'Farrell, who also did the original survey of San Francisco. With the survey in hand, Semple got down to the business of selling lots. In addition to proposed streets and lots, the first survey included a "Military Reservation" to the east of the town.[21,22]

In 1886, Hubert Howe Bancroft described Vallejo's motives for selling to Semple. He said, "Vallejo's chief motive was to increase the value of his remaining lands, by promoting the settlement of the northern frontier."[23]

## THE MILITARY RESERVATION AT BENICIA
## COMES TO RANCHO SUSCOL

With the conclusion of the Mexican War in 1846, U.S. Navy and Army forces occupied the new territory and established bases of operation. One was the Presidio of San Francisco, which was a collection of adobe buildings established by the Spanish. From the presidio, officials searched the West Coast for appropriate locations for logistical and operational bases.

At the age of twenty-three, recent West Point graduate Lieutenant James A. Hardie was sent to California in 1846 to help organize the army on the Pacific coast. He was named as a temporary major and joined the Third Artillery Regiment in San Francisco. With Lieutenant William T. Sherman, Hardie selected the Presidio of San Francisco as the administrative headquarters and Benicia as a military reservation and logistical base for the West Coast and the Pacific. Sherman did the first survey of the reservation. The city of San Francisco was thought to be inappropriate for a logistical base because of the high price of land and the vulnerability of the peninsula to invasion. Semple offered the land free of charge, seeing an opportunity to advance his development of Benicia. The site at Benicia was decided upon as early as 1847 because of this deal and the strategic location on the Carquinez Straits that linked the bay to the California interior.[24]

While cavalry and infantry units populated the land at Benicia Point as early as 1847, Brevet Lieutenant Colonel Silas E. Casey of the Second Infantry Regiment became the founder and first commanding officer of the army outpost when he founded "the post at Point near Benicia" on April 30, 1849. Simultaneously, the Benicia Quartermaster Depot was established and wooden quarters for both infantry and cavalry units were constructed.[25]

The land was transferred directly from General Vallejo, Semple, Larkin and Phelps and appears as a "Military Reservation" on the first 1847 survey. During the 117 years that they coexisted, the city never tried to incorporate the Arsenal property into the city boundaries, an issue that would have to be resolved when the reservation closed in 1964.[26]

## JOHN FRISBIE AND THE CITY OF VALLEJO

Colonel John Frisbie was born in Albany, New York, on May 10, 1823. He and Leland Stanford studied law with a prominent lawyer in Albany, and Frisbie subsequently enjoyed a lucrative practice there. In 1846, he was elected captain of the Van Rensselaer Guard, which was a militia unit. During the Mexican War, Frisbie recruited a company that joined the New York Volunteers for duty in California. He arrived in San Francisco on March 5, 1847, and was given command of the Sonoma barracks in 1848. This is where he met the Vallejo family. After his discharge, Frisbie persuaded Mariano Vallejo to open dry goods stores in Sonoma, Napa and Benicia. While not a delegate, Frisbie took part as a legal consultant in the California constitutional convention of 1849, which was held in Monterey.[27]

In 1850, Vallejo gave Frisbie power of attorney over Rancho Suscol. This allowed Frisbie to bargain, grant and sell land on Rancho Suscol, and Frisbie did sell a large amount to investors in San Francisco. Frisbie and Vallejo created the new city of Vallejo, with Frisbie executing the actual legal documents and sales in the project. On April 3, 1851, Frisbie married Epifania, the oldest and favorite daughter of General Vallejo and his secretary in later life. While Frisbie was occupied with many business dealings, he coordinated the defense of his and Vallejo's land titles involving several ranchos. Frisbie and other investors started the Vallejo Water Company and the Vallejo Land and Improvement Company, which subdivided and developed Vallejo into a modern city.[28]

## VALLEJO PROVES HIS TITLE TO RANCHO SUSCOL

Land ownership was a key political battle of nineteenth-century California. At the end of the Mexican War, Mexico and the United States finalized the Treaty of Guadalupe Hidalgo. Part of the treaty was a clause recognizing legitimate land claims in the former Mexican lands. Congress established a land commission to judge the legitimacy of each claim, and General Vallejo's Rancho Suscol became case 318ND. Vallejo petitioned the land commission in San Francisco by submitting certified and translated copies of the following documents:

1. A handwritten map.
2. A colonization grant to Vallejo dated March 15, 1843, signed by Governor Micheltorena and countersigned by Francisco Arce as secretary *ad interim*.
3. Another grant dated June 19, 1844, reciting that Vallejo had requested the purchase of the tract for the sum of $5,000, that the governor had sold it to him for that sum and declared him to be the owner of the land without restriction. This paper also purported to be signed and countersigned by Micheltorena and Arce.
4. A certificate dated December 26, 1845, signed by Pio Pico, as governor, and attested by Jose Maria Covarrubias, setting forth that both grants had been approved by the Departmental Assembly on September 26, 1845.
5. A letter dated March 16, 1843, which was addressed to Colonel G. Mariano Vallejo, military commandant of the line from Santa Juez to Sonoma, signed by Micheltorena and sealed with the seal of the Departmental Government. This letter

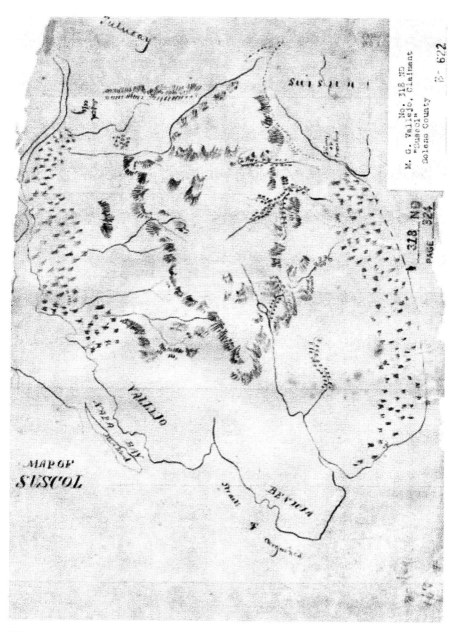

*Diseño*, or map, of Rancho Suscol that was used to support Vallejo's land claim, circa 1850. *Courtesy Benicia Historical Museum.*

purported to document that the Rancho Nacional Suscol was transferred from the Mexican government to Vallejo in trade for goods and silver.

6. Letters and documents supporting the claim and documenting that Vallejo was using the land.[29]

The land commission validated Vallejo's claim in 1855. It turned out to be just the beginning of the battle for Vallejo and Frisbie.

## LITIGATION

People started coming into California looking for land. Many came to establish farms but couldn't locate farmland that was free for the taking. They settled without ownership or permission on lands owned by the *Californios* and the original settlers, such as Frisbie and Semple. Called "squatters" by the land owners, these immigrants from the eastern United States mostly settled on lands adjacent to the trails through the Sierra Nevada Mountains leading to the San Francisco Bay Area. San Francisco and its adjoining towns were a rich market for farm goods. When squatters began settling on Rancho Suscol, including Benicia, General Vallejo reacted by creating his own private army from the remnants of the Patwin and Miwok peoples and headed by the extremely tall Chief Solano. The resulting land war would rage for twenty years.[30]

The Americans pouring into California resented the fact that vast sections of prime land were locked up in huge ranchos like Suscol. There was a large push to break up the ranchos, despite the promises in the Treaty of Guadalupe Hidalgo. After substantial lobbying in Washington, D.C., the U.S. attorney for Northern California filed suit against Vallejo, alleging that the title to Rancho Suscol was not legal. With Frisbie representing Vallejo, the case was tried in 1856 before the United States District Court for Northern California in the city of San Francisco. Rancho Suscol was not the only rancho targeted. Dozens of ranchos that had been certified by the land commission as being the legitimate property of the *Californios* were the subject of litigation, and many families lost their property as a result.

The case of *United States v. Vallejo* went to trial in San Francisco before a federal judge. The United States argued that neither of the grants were referenced in the Mexican catalogue of land grants or recorded in the *Toma de Razon*, a Mexican record of governmental proceedings. No documents were found on the grant or the purchase in any Mexican government file. The journals of the Departmental Assembly showed that the grants were not presented before that body either on September 26, 1845, as alleged in a letter from former Mexican governor Pio Pico, or any other day.[31]

Three witnesses for the government testified that they knew the land called the Rancho Nacional Suscol and that it was occupied by soldiers of the Mexican army until the time of the American conquest. A Mr. Watson swore that in 1848 he proposed to purchase part of the land from Vallejo and was told that the land was purchased from the Suscol Indians, but Vallejo expected the United States government would swindle him out of it and refused, for that reason, to sell with a warranty of title.[32]

Frisbie, by then Vallejo's son-in-law, produced several witnesses who supported Vallejo's position. J.B.R. Cooper, a highly respected businessman and former *alcalde* of Sonoma, testified that he was captain of the schooner *California* that transported Vallejo's goods from Petaluma to San Diego. Cooper also said that Governor Micheltorena told him that Vallejo had offered twenty thousand silver Spanish dollars for Rancho Nacional Suscol and that the goods were to go in payment.[33]

Four witnesses testified that Vallejo occupied Rancho Suscol for his own purposes after the purchase from the Mexican government. Vallejo produced a deposition of Pablo de la Guerra, a respected Santa Barbara Don, who declared that he knew the handwriting of Governor Manuel Micheltorena and his secretary, Francisco Arce, and their signatures on the two grants were genuine. Micheltorena had returned to Mexico after the American conquest, but Arce was still in California and was not called by Vallejo's attorneys. Vallejo's attorneys introduced a deposition from I.D. Marks, who testified to conversations in Mexico in which Micheltorena told him that he had extraordinary powers as governor and that his acts had been approved. Marks also testified that Jose Fernando Reyes, secretary of state of Mexico, said that the full powers to grant lands in California had been delegated to Micheltorena by General Santa Anna under the *Bases of Tacubaya*.[34]

Vallejo prevailed in the district court, having proven that the land purchase and land grant were legal under Mexican law and that Vallejo had taken all the necessary steps to make them legal under U.S. law. The case was appealed by the U.S. attorney and went to the court of appeals, which was also in San Francisco. The court quickly upheld the lower court decision that Vallejo legally owned the land.

## TO THE SUPREME COURT

The U.S. Supreme Court saw the matter differently. In a decision in 1861, the Supreme Court said that there was no official record of the transaction under Mexican law; therefore, the grants and sale of land were not legally upheld by the land commission. The case led to the "Suscol principle," which stated that all documents had to be complete and fully in compliance with Mexican law for a claim to be valid. The decision resulted in the ownership of the former Rancho Nacional Suscol reverting to the United States government. The action made thousands of land titles in the former rancho invalid, including that of the Benicia Arsenal. The Suscol principle would influence litigation of land grant claims for the remainder of the century. The last case was finally adjudicated by the Supreme Court in 1943.[35]

The army secured the Benicia Arsenal property immediately with a letter from President Abraham Lincoln, which read,

> *Executive Mansion.*
> *Washington City, October 7th, 1862*
> *In conformity with the request of the Secretary of War of this date, it is hereby ordered that a plot of land at Benicia, in the State of California, described in a certain diagram now on file in the office of the Deputy Quartermaster General at San Francisco in the abovementioned State, be segregated from the public lands for a Military Reservation; and the Secretary of the Interior is hereby directed to take such action as will secure the object and purpose herein set forth.*
> */s/ A. Lincoln*
> *President of the United States*
> *Hon. Caleb B. Smith*
> *Secretary of the Interior.[36]*

## PREEMPTION

The ownership of the people who purchased portions of Rancho Suscol from Vallejo, Frisbie or Semple was in jeopardy. As news of the Supreme Court decision spread, more squatters came into Rancho Suscol and challenged the titles of the people who had legally purchased property. The issue of land ownership preemption was not new to Congress. The concept is that land from a previous regime could preempt the title to the land over others coming into the area. Owners of land in former British, French and Spanish territories (and later Russian and Hawaiian territories) could preempt their lands from use by subsequent immigrants.

Frisbie immediately acted through Timothy Phelps, California's member of the House of Representatives, to introduce a preemption act specific to California in 1862. The act would have guaranteed title to the settlers who already owned the land at the time of the Supreme Court decision, thus freezing out the squatters and ensuring the land titles of those settlers and investors who had purchased the land legally from General Vallejo. The act failed because politicians on the East Coast wanted acreage limits and politicians on the West Coast did not. Rather than be encumbered with acreage limits, the proponents delayed the bill.[37]

## Land War: The Settlers Bring in the Regulators to Remove the Squatters

The Supreme Court decision and the failure of the preemption bill created a void because the land ownership reverted to the United States, but no federal agency was present to take charge of the land, and there was no law or system in place to deal with land ownership in the former rancho. In the year following the Supreme Court decision, 189 squatters flowed into the former rancho, erecting sheds, stringing up barbed wire fencing and building homes. The response from Frisbie and Vallejo was to step up the campaign against the squatters. They brought in people they called regulators, who were hired guns to remove the squatters. Tough, hardened men, many of the regulators were veterans or deserters from the Union and Confederate armies. They were heavily armed and conducted midnight raids and shootings and threatened the squatters. Despite the saber rattling, it appears that nobody was actually hurt in the land war. That wasn't Frisbie's style. In his mind, threats and bribes did the job. Frisbie also initiated and won twelve lawsuits in federal and state courts to protect his rights to Suscol and other lands affected by the Supreme Court decision and squatter encroachments.[38]

In 1863, Congressman Phelps introduced another preemption bill before Congress—this time with no limits on acreage. It passed, thus guaranteeing the titles of the settlers and investors on Rancho Suscol and freezing out the squatters. The settlers celebrated with a *fandango* at Suscol House, where more than one thousand guests of Frisbie and his partners enjoyed beef, vegetables and copious amounts of alcohol.[39]

The land war heated up. The investors and settlers hired more regulators to terrorize the squatters into leaving the land. Many did leave, and others accepted cash or land bribes to leave. The federal land commissioners also tried to charge landowners in Benicia and Vallejo more money than those in the rest of the rancho to patent (deed) their lands. The Benicia City Council hired attorney Lansing Mizner, a cousin of Robert Semple, who was renowned for selling underwater lots. He petitioned Congress, asking that landowners in the cities be charged the same low price as those in the countryside. It worked.[40]

Over the next three decades, the federal government wrote hundreds of patents for properties in the former Rancho Suscol and other ranchos in California. The patents were duly recorded in the Solano County recorder's office and can be viewed there in seven leather-bound volumes. The last patent was issued, and the Rancho Suscol case finally closed, in 1893.

# 3
# Monterey

## The California Constitutional Convention

While the land disputes were raging throughout California, the fact that by 1849 the area was a military department and not a state or a territory hindered a resolution of the problem. Real estate law became a mixture of the Mexican and American systems. Criminal law disintegrated into vigilante actions, not only in San Francisco but also in the farms and mines. Civil law was decided by local *alcaldes* under the Mexican system, and the Mother Lode area developed its own system to manage claims. A carryover from the Spanish and Mexican systems of government, *alcaldes* were appointed by the governor, who, after 1846, were American generals who governed as part judge, part mayor and part recorder. Congress was locked in a battle over slavery, and no decision was forthcoming. Some Americans in California, the self-styled Chivs, were talking about their own country.

## CALIFORNIA: THE "CHIVS"

Slavery was an issue that would haunt California until the Thirteenth Amendment passed in 1865. It was not an abstract issue in California politics or in Benicia. Down the street from the new Benicia Presbyterian church resided slave Adam Willis, the property of Singleton Vaughn. At the time, slaves were purchased, owned and sold under the state and federal property laws. The decade of the 1840s witnessed a steady influx of slaves into California from the east and the establishment of an underground railroad to free them. What happened to the Presbyterian church provides a metaphor for what was happening to the country.

Religion—the great driving political force of nineteenth-century America—took sides in the slavery issue. The Presbyterians shattered into what they termed the Old School and the New School. The New School Presbyterians joined the abolitionist Congregational or Methodist churches. The Old School Presbyterians didn't come out as a body directly in support of slavery, though some of the members owned slaves. They had a firm policy of noninterference with the civil authorities on the issue. As the debates over slavery festered and began to be linked with secession, the Old School assembly also kept a hands-off attitude, while many of its members publicly spoke in favor of slavery and secession. Thus, the Old School Presbyterians were painted with a broad brush as supporting both.[41]

Secession was a real issue in California politics. In May 1851, the Democratic Party held its annual convention at the Benicia Presbyterian church. It was an opportunity for politicians to meet all the major players in California politics. The convention started the process for the "Southern Chivalry" or "Chivs" to take control of the state government.

Men from the South, and many of them slave owners, the Chivs gained powerful footholds in the legislature, governor's office and courts. Among other things, they passed the Fugitive Slave Act, denied black people the ability to testify against white people in court and attempted to pass legislation supporting the Confederacy.[42]

The Chivs evolved into the California Breckinridge Democratic Party in 1860 in support of John C. Breckinridge for president of the United States. The election of 1861, when the Republican Party gained control of the California governor's office and the legislature, derailed their plans to gain control of the state for the Confederacy. The sobering lists of the dead from the eastern battlefields and the Thirteenth Amendment to the U.S. Constitution eventually destroyed both the Chivs and the Breckinridge Democrats forever. But in 1849, they were a force to be reckoned with.

## THE MONTEREY CONVENTION

When the Monterey Convention started in 1849, California had already been in limbo for three years, and there was no end in sight. The chain of events leading to the convention started in 1836 when the Republic of Texas declared independence from Mexico. The push for Texas to join the Union was intense in Washington, D.C. James K. Polk (1785–1849), presidential candidate in 1844, tied the Texas annexation to the ongoing Oregon dispute and won election on an expansionist platform. Before Polk took office, Congress approved the annexation of Texas on April 24, 1846, which led to the outbreak of the Mexican-American War. Congress declared war against Mexico on May 13, 1846.[43]

The U.S. Navy Pacific Squadron captured Monterey and Yerba Buena (later San Francisco) in July 1846. By the end of the year, United States naval and ground forces had secured California, and hostilities, such as they were, ended with the Treaty of Cahuenga on January 13, 1847.

Then began a three-year occupation under a succession of military governors. The military government was ineffectual because of the small number of troops available and their constant desertion. Local governments, such as Benicia, resorted to *alcaldes* under a hybrid of the U.S. and Mexican systems. Nevertheless, California began to disintegrate into chaos as gangs of bandits and pirates proliferated and raided farms, ships, stage lines and everything else. Land claims and ownership were in chaos, and many old *Californio* families complained of squatters setting up ranches on their lands.

The Treaty of Guadalupe Hidalgo formally ended the war and ceded California to the United States on July 4, 1848. The treaty gave the United States a legal basis for occupying California but didn't settle the issue of governance. When gold was discovered at Sutter's Mill on January 24, 1848, and announced to the world from San Francisco the following March, matters only became more acute.[44]

The government in Washington, D.C., suddenly saw California as a cash cow and more than a collection of dusty ranchos. Throughout the remainder of 1848, and especially through 1849, thousands of argonauts streamed into California looking for gold or looking to "mine the miners." The governmental chaos only increased as miners took the law into their own hands and land sales were stalled.

Washington, D.C., was increasingly occupied with the issue of slavery. Congress and the president had tried to keep a delicate balance between Southern proslavery forces and the northern Free-Soilers, who didn't want

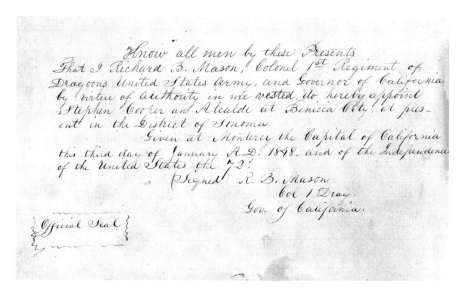

Document appointing Stephen Cooper *alcalde* of Benicia on January 3, 1848. *Courtesy Benicia Historical Museum.*

to see slavery spread to the potential new states in the West and Northwest. There was also the idea of territorial balance, in which the size of a territory or state would be balanced so that one state wouldn't overwhelm another. However, that had already been disrupted by the annexation of Texas.

There were laws on the books laying out the process for a state to form. Starting with the Northwest Ordinance of the Confederation Congress—under the Articles of Confederation—in 1784, a process was outlined to create new states. The process basically included a minimum population of free persons, a scientific survey of the land, a period of territoriality when a territorial government was formed, basic governmental services and a constitution. However, Washington, D.C., was mired in indecision from the battle over slavery, and California was sliding into chaos as the Chivs lobbied for legal slavery.[45]

Frontier duty for the U.S. Army included topographical surveys, veterinary care, law enforcement, medical care, emergency relief and keeping the peace. But the army was not organized to run a state. The military governor of California, General Bennett C. Riley, stepped into the situation and took charge. Responding to multiple requests from *Californio* residents and U.S. immigrants—and realizing the futility of a military government—Riley issued an official proclamation on June 3, 1849, calling for a constitutional convention and an election of representatives.[46]

*Left*: Colton Hall in Monterey, California, circa 1860. *Courtesy California Department of Parks and Recreation.*

*Below*: First page of the 1849 California Constitution. *Courtesy California State Archives.*

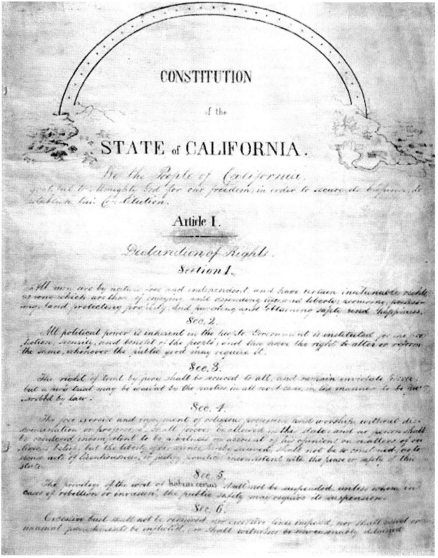

The representatives were elected by secret ballot. The forty-eight delegates were mostly pre-1846 settlers and included eight *Californios*, who necessitated Spanish interpreters. Solano County, where Benicia is located, was represented by General Guadalupe M. Vallejo and Robert Semple, who would be elected president of the convention.[47]

Once elected president, Semple campaigned to have Benicia designated as the state capital, and the debate over the location became heated. Many delegates argued for Monterey, as it was the obvious choice. An established town and capital of Spanish and Mexican California, it had restaurants, lodgings and the extremely important archives. Colton Hall, where the delegates were meeting, was readily available as a meeting place for the legislature, and there were former Mexican offices available for the governor and other officers. However, the gold rush had dramatically changed the population patterns in the state, and the population center had shifted to the gold fields. Gold was ultimately responsible for Monterey losing the capital. Most delegates believed that the capital should be close to the center of the action—the gold mines. As Walter Colton remarked in his diary, "It is not in a man to raise cabbages in a soil that contains gold." San Jose was a compromise and was designated in the constitution as the first capital.[48,49]

The constitution was completed and signed on October 13, 1849, and was rushed out for ratification by public vote before the rainy season began. The vote became a plebiscite for union with the United States. On Election Day, November 13, 1849, the weather was terrible in California, and the turnout was light. Nevertheless, the vote went to the constitution and, by sentiment, to the Union. General Riley issued a military proclamation recognizing the state as a duly constituted legal body, and California was up and running as a state in the fall of 1849—a year before becoming a state of the United States.[50]

# 4

# San Jose

## The State's First Capital

The 1849 state constitution called for the legislature to meet in the Pueblo de San Jose and then to determine, by law, where to meet from then on. Mud-sodden roads kept most of the senators and assemblymen from arriving for the first week. While the first legislature consisted of sixteen senators and thirty-six assemblymen, only six senators arrived on the first day of what was destined to be labeled the "Legislature of a Thousand Drinks" because most of the business of the state was carried out in the adjacent taverns. What they found was less than adequate. Despite the desperate efforts of San Jose's citizens to prepare, there was a severe lack of lodgings and the so-called state hall was nothing more than a forty-by-sixty-foot unfinished wood box. Price gouging was rampant, and the expenses of living were enormous and were not covered by the sixteen dollar per diem the legislators received. Five dollars in gold paid for a flea-infested, vermin-ridden, dirt floor lodging with leaking ceilings. Not that this was any different from any of the other lodgings outside of San Francisco. All of California was known for its bedbugs and fleas.[51]

On December 20, 1849, General Riley signed a proclamation officially surrendering the leadership of the state to Peter H. Burnett, who became California's first governor. In quick order, John C. Frémont and William Gwin were elected as U.S. senators and dispatched to Washington, D.C., to lobby for statehood. The various offices and courts were organized, and basic laws were written. In all manners, the legislature and governor acted as if California were a legally constituted state that was part of the Union.[52]

Bronze plaque located at Cesar Chavez Park in San Jose celebrating the location of the first California capitol in 2019. *Courtesy Reg Page.*

No one was happy in San Jose. As the winter legislative session progressed, so did the rains and mud as Coyote Creek overflowed. The deluge virtually trapped the state government, such as it was at the time, in the *pueblo*. On December 4, 1849, the Monterey delegation was authorized to offer the use of Colton Hall. The delegation from San Francisco also lobbied for their town, which had the advantage of multiple suitable lodgings. Other delegations lobbied for Sacramento, Santa Barbara and Stockton. David Broderick, who would later become a U.S. senator before he was murdered in a duel over slavery, was appointed the chair of a committee to search for a new capital site. Bills were proposed and withdrawn, there were heated conversations and debates and money changed hands.[53]

Colonel Jonathan D. Stevenson, who commanded the New York Volunteers as they sailed around Cape Horn in 1847 to support Frémont's Battalion, made an impassioned plea for the "New York of the Pacific" at the head of the Bay of Suisun, where the Sacramento and San Joaquin Rivers joined. At first it was unclear whether he was talking of Vallejo, Benicia or Stockton. However, in subsequent newspaper articles and speeches, Walter Colton, the *alcalde* of Monterey, and Stevenson made it clear that they were talking about a new city bounded by the San Joaquin and Sacramento Rivers and the Carquinez Straits. This was never to be, and today the area remains a sea of tule reeds.[54]

As a counter, the people of San Jose made a significant offer of free land and money for a capitol and state offices. They pointed out that the land title was solid and the best in the state—particularly as compared to Rancho Suscol, where a leading contender, Benicia, was located. Sacramento representatives argued that their land titles were also solid and that they already had a lot of land claimed for subdivisions. Monterey came back and offered all of its municipal buildings in addition to Colton Hall. It also proposed a botanical garden or model farm, a workhouse and a prison on one thousand acres of public land.[55]

## General Vallejo Steps in With an Offer the State Couldn't Refuse

On April 3, 1850, G. Mariano Vallejo made a fabulous offer. Through his son-in-law, John Frisbie, General Vallejo proposed to give the state land and money for a capitol; a governor's house; offices for the comptroller, treasurer, secretary of state, surveyor general and nine other officers; a library; an orphans' asylum; a charity hospital for men and women; an asylum for the blind; a lunatic asylum; common schools; a botanical garden; and a penitentiary. The state could even call the new capital city any name it wanted and suggested "Eureka" as an example. Vallejo also argued that the location was perfect because it was on land and water routes between San Francisco and the interior, including the gold fields.[56]

David C. Broderick, the chairman of the Committee on Public Buildings and Grounds, presented a long report supporting Vallejo's proposition. He especially liked the idea that the area, present-day Vallejo, was on a waterway and easily accessible to other parts of the state—especially San Francisco, Stockton and Sacramento. The proposition passed the senate and the assembly. However, when the matter went to Governor Burnett, he called for a public referendum to make the decision. In the spring of 1850, Sacramento businessmen saw an opportunity and started planning to present Sacramento as the capital site.[57]

Referencing the sacking of Washington, D.C., just thirty-two years prior, the *Alta California*, California's major newspaper, published several long editorials that suggested San Jose would be safer from foreign invasion than

Monterey, the city of Vallejo or "New York" (referring to the undeveloped location at the confluence of the Sacramento and San Joaquin Rivers).[58]

On September 9, 1850, the president of the United States, Millard Fillmore, signed the bill that made California the thirty-first state. The following day, the U.S. Senate accepted the credentials of William M. Gwin and John C. Frémont and administered the oaths of office. California heard the news on October 18, 1850, when the *USS Oregon* sailed into San Francisco Bay. The state government continued with no changes.[59]

The general state election to decide the location of the capital, the first election since becoming an actual state in the Union, was held on October 7, 1850. The City of Vallejo won with 7,477 votes, while Benicia received 70.[60]

TABLE 1. VOTES OF THE GENERAL STATE ELECTION ON OCTOBER 7, 1850

| | |
|---|---|
| Vallejo | 7,477 |
| San Jose | 1,292 |
| San Diego | 14 |
| Monterey | 399 |
| Santa Cruz | 2 |
| Reed's Proposition | 651 |
| Gilroy | 71 |
| Eureka | 301 |
| Stockton | 6 |
| Sacramento | 160 |
| San Francisco | 25 |
| Benicia | 70 |
| Nevada | 82 |
| Downieville | 150 |
| Hamilton | 10 |
| Long's Bar | 1 |
| Nicolaus | 1 |
| Stuart's Bar | 1 |
| Yuba City | 14 |
| Marysville | 1 |
| Trinidad City | 1 |

*"The California State Register and Yearbook of Facts: 1859," San Francisco: Henry G. Longley and Samuel A. Morison, 1859.*

General Vallejo traveled to San Jose from his home in Sonoma to present his ideas for a capital at his proposed site. On January 14, 1851, Martin E. Cooke proposed in the senate that General Vallejo was prepared to execute a bond for the fulfillment of the proposition he made to the previous legislature. On January 16, a resolution was submitted by Martin Cooke to request a report from the surveyor general on the various proposed locations for the seat of government. The motion stalled as opposition to the Vallejo site mounted from Sacramento and San Francisco advocates. A rear guard action by the San Jose contingent committed to donating $406,000 worth of land.[61]

The fight spilled over into the assembly but was stifled when General Vallejo submitted his bond. The bond, essentially an agreement, was a five-page document that laid out what the City of Vallejo promised to provide, including a statehouse and other state offices. There was a bitter debate in the newspaper editorial pages, the legislature and, presumably, the taverns, where most of the business of state was conducted.[62]

Despite the statewide vote, Vallejo's bond crept through the legislature. Three commissioners were appointed from the senate and the assembly to travel to Vallejo to select the plots of land. San Jose continued its rear guard opposition to the move, and Monterey came forward with a serious sticking point. The archives of the Spanish and Mexican governments were in Monterey and were in poor condition. Further, the records of the California constitutional convention were still there. These archives did not travel well and were important for proving land ownership claims and other legal issues from the Spanish and Mexican periods. Nothing was decided for the moment.[63]

As to be expected from the Legislature of a Thousand Drinks, money changed hands. A lot of money, as reported by the *Alta California* on May 27, 1851: "The Great Bargain by which the State Capital was taken away from the habitations of men and located among the coyotes is to be consummated on the 10th of June prox. Originally the whole affair was a bribe and a bargain, in which the offer of $375,000 bought the votes of the State."[64]

In June 1851, Governor John McDougal ordered the public archives be moved from San Jose to Vallejo. However, when it was discovered that the accommodations in Vallejo were not even begun, he ordered the documents be sent back to San Jose.[65]

By December of the same year, matters were looking better. James S. Graham, the superintendent of public buildings, informed Governor McDougal that he had visited Vallejo and found the statehouse,

*An excellent and beautiful building and superior to any yet occupied by the Legislature. The buildings intended for the State officers are not so good as those occupied at San Jose, but sufficiently progressed for the reception of Public officers and amply sufficient for the transaction of public business.*[66]

## SAN FRANCISCO:
## A QUICK MEETING OF THE LEGISLATURE

To finally settle the issue of where the state capital should be located, the members-elect of the legislature met in San Francisco on December 30, 1851. San Francisco had two advantages over San Jose at this time: San Jose was choked in mud as it usually was that time of year, and San Francisco boasted plenty of lodgings and—most importantly—taverns. That San Francisco wasn't chosen for the capital is a mystery, though there were drawbacks, including the high land prices and vulnerability to foreign attack. Sacramento had a strong group working for the capital, but the City of Vallejo had won the election, after all. All the legislators agreed on Vallejo.[67]

# 5

# Vallejo

## The Second Capital of California

The third session of the legislature convened in Vallejo on January 5, 1852, and the members were immediately dissatisfied. The place was a mess, and worse, it was a lie. The capitol was an incomplete shack. The lodgings were worse than San Jose, with chairs and only a few beds for the legislators. The only thing of use in the city at the time was the long wharf. At least there was no mud, but there was also not enough food or water. As Mary G. Kos wrote, "The members, as a whole, were extremely dissatisfied. Their seats were temporary benches, made of boards placed on stools and nail kegs, and the benches frequently gave way which was a trifle hard on senatorial dignity!"[68]

The issues of the legality of General Vallejo's title claims to Rancho Suscol, the Mexican rancho on which the cities of Vallejo and Benicia stood, were again raised. It became immediately clear that General Vallejo had not lived up to his promises, and the legislature decamped en masse. Later, the building was destroyed by fire and is now commemorated by a memorial plaque at the corner of York and Sacramento Streets in Vallejo.

Within just two days, on January 7, 1852, Governor John McDougal submitted an official objection to meeting in Vallejo. Given General Vallejo's inability to meet his promises, nobody was surprised. When John Bigler took the oath of office and became governor the following day, he joined the legislature in expressing dissatisfaction with the town and General Vallejo. Sacramento seemed the logical alternate, especially given the fact that San Jose was once again isolated in a sea of mud as Coyote Creek overflowed its banks.[69]

CAPITOL AT VALLEJO—1852-1853.

The capitol in Vallejo. *Courtesy Benicia Historical Museum.*

Sacramento City had a lot to offer the state government. It was the second-largest city in California; it was laid out in a grid pattern; it was adjacent to the extremely lucrative gold mines and agricultural fields; and, most importantly, it had plenty of lodgings and taverns. It even had theaters—a rarity on the frontier. The city was a boomtown in a state full of them and was ready to donate its county courthouse to the state. But there was a problem. Like San Jose, it was prone to flooding and often turned into mud flats in the spring.

In Vallejo, the legislature began another bitter debate. Sacramento was proposed and defeated. An ever-shrinking pro-Vallejo contingent reminded the group that the voters had chosen Vallejo. San Jose advocates countered that General Vallejo had reneged on his promises. Other towns, including San Jose, San Francisco and nearby, Benicia lobbied. Something had to be done before the fleas and bedbugs devoured the state government, or worse, the archives were damaged.[70]

On January 12, 1852, a pro-Sacramento resolution passed both houses of the legislature, and the legislators immediately adjourned to meet in the "River

City" on January 16—a Friday. The state chartered a steamer, the *Eureka*, and everyone, along with the furniture and documents, departed for Sacramento. It was a partial victory for the supporters of a Sacramento capital. If only temporarily, they had the upper hand. The citizens of San Jose, under J.D. Hoppe, petitioned for a restraining order, claiming their city was the legal seat of government. The injunction was served, but the legislature dissolved it by a joint motion. On January 21, the state archives arrived in Sacramento from Monterey, with a shipping cost of $616.50 ($154,125 in 2019 dollars).[71]

## SACRAMENTO:
## THE TEMPORARY SEAT OF GOVERNMENT

Sacramento would be the temporary seat of government from January 16, 1852, to May 4, 1852. The citizens of Sacramento created a slush fund by collecting $20 in gold from each city booster and threw a party on the evening of January 16. The hospitality continued with wining, dining, theaters and, presumably, other entertainments in the red-light district that stretched along the Sacramento and American Rivers. The purpose, of course, was to draw a sharp distinction between Sacramento—the party city—and San Jose and Vallejo—the mud cities. The citizens of Vallejo cried foul in a series of petitions to the legislature. They argued that they had been left with construction and other expenses for the capital city and made claims of $87,638 against the state. They also had problems finding enough room for the whole state government in the Sacramento City Hall.[72]

In February 1852, a message was received by the legislature from the mayor and the Benicia City Council, offering itself as the state capital:

> *The undersigned Mayor and Council of the City of Benicia, believing that the question of the permanent location of the State Capital will be finally determined during the present session of the Legislature, and feeling deeply interested in the decision of the question, would respectfully represent, (in case a removal from the City of Vallejo shall be determined upon), to the consideration of the Legislature now assembled, the propriety of selecting as the permanent Capital of the State, the City of Benicia, in Solano County. The city of Benicia is suitably, centrally and conveniently located on the great thoroughfare, to the interior of the State and can be reached by land, or water, at all seasons of the year.*

The following March, the legislature received a resolution from the mayor and council of San Francisco offering the Fog City, as San Francisco is known, as the site of the capital. San Jose still wanted what it considered its rightful place as capital. Then in March, Sacramento flooded for three days when the American River breached the levees. After the flooding receded and the legislators returned, the Court of Sessions of Sacramento offered the courthouse to the legislature for the next session, and a citizen's group pledged a considerable amount of land for permanent buildings. Monterey again lobbied to return the capital to the traditional location.[73]

Nevertheless, Vallejo had been designated capital of the state by a plebiscite. The *Daily Alta California* reported on May 12, 1852, "We learn that the Superintendent of Public Buildings, Col. Graham, is to take steps any day to have the State furniture, now in the courthouse at Sacramento, removed to Vallejo, and used to fit up the Senate Chamber, Hall of the assembly, committee rooms & of the capitol building."[74]

## VALLEJO: THE SECOND TRY

While the legislature was still meeting in Sacramento, lobbying by General Vallejo and Colonel Frisbie worked, and the legislature passed an act on April 30, 1852, recognizing Vallejo as the permanent seat of the state government. The archives and state officers were directed to move there. On May 4, 1852, the legislature adjourned with an intention to meet in Vallejo the following January, leaving the citizens of Vallejo seven months to do some serious construction.[75]

When the legislature convened in Vallejo on January 3, 1853, conditions had not appreciably improved. The buildings were nothing more than ramshackle shacks. The food and lodging situations were even worse as more legislators and state staff flooded the city. The narrow benches that substituted for chairs in the capitol were uncomfortable and completely unusable. As with most of California, the town was overrun by fleas and bedbugs. The steamboat *Empire* was moored to the city wharf and served as a floating hotel. The *Sacramento Daily Union* announced satirically, "Vallejo is certainly a magnificent seat for the capital of the State of California."[76]

Benica was only a short buggy ride away from Vallejo and was poised to take advantage of the misery of the situation. It had taverns and hotels—though not as many as Sacramento; a wharf; and, most importantly, a newly minted city hall, where the state government could meet. All of the river steamships stopped in Benicia on their way to and from Sacramento, Stockton and San Francisco. The mayor of Benicia sent another letter to the legislature on behalf of the city council and offered the use of the city hall as a statehouse. Other cities kept up the pressure, especially Monterey, which again offered Colton Hall. Sacramento was temporarily taken out of the running when a massive fire destroyed most of the businesses, including the lodgings and all-important taverns—both necessary for the proper functioning of the government. A committee was appointed to study the situation again.[77]

Debate over the location of the capital preoccupied the legislature for another month, leaving little time for other issues. On January 27, S.C. Hastings, the attorney general, settled the plebiscite that selected Vallejo as the capital when he issued an inquiry from the assembly stating, "The future disposition of the Seat of Government, is subject to the control of the legislature, like any other subject of legislation." That same day, General Vallejo backed out of the deal, offering land but nothing else.[78]

The state government was not going to let General Vallejo off so easily. He had committed to paying for the state expenses of moving to Vallejo, so on February 4, Governor Bigler sent him a bill for $375,000 for "all moneys that may be now due." One can presume that Vallejo choked on the bill when he saw it. He responded that he needed to consult with his lawyers—meaning his son-in-law, John B. Frisbie. That same day, the assembly and the state senate passed resolutions to adjourn, with the intention to meet in Benicia on the February 11. The "act to provide for the permanent location of the Seat of Government" was immediately signed by Governor Bigler, and the archives were ordered transferred to Benicia.[79]

# 6

# Benicia

## The City Council and the Mayor Make an Offer

The Benicia City Council met for the first time on May 7, 1850, five months before California statehood and following a short period of the provisional council. The main topic of conversation was the need for a city hall, and from the beginning, the council and businessmen of the city were intent on moving the state capital to Benicia. In the meantime, the city leased a building on First Street from Benjamin Barlow to be used as a city hall. As early as July 1851, the proposed city hall was being referred to as the state capitol: "We are informed by the Benicia press that the state capitol, a few miles down the Bay, is not yet finished."[80,81]

The council started writing bylaws and organized itself into a series of committees. The emphasis was on building streets, wharves and sewers. The council also acted as the city's first board of education, hiring Sylvester Woodbridge as its first teacher. In June, the committee on improvements proposed a "gaol" be constructed. There was an issue of animal carcasses appearing on First Street and a need for their immediate removal. A contract was made with Dr. Peabody to treat paupers at his hospital for a fee of $3.50 per day.[82]

At a meeting on May 17, 1851, problems with the council's meeting room popped up. The monthly rent of $125 was too high, the lighting was bad and the owner of the furniture demanded payment. A committee was formed to find a suitable alternative site, but no acceptable replacement could be found. So, another lease was signed at a higher rate, and the furniture was purchased and paid for by the sale of bonds.[83]

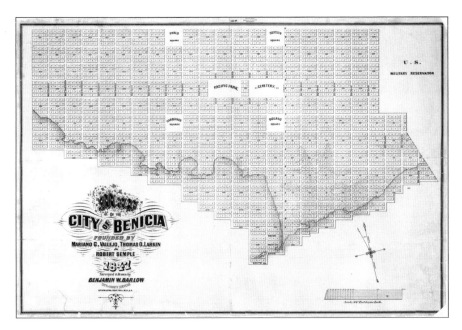

First map of Benicia, 1847. *Courtesy City of Benicia.*

Several other issues were coming before Benicia, including water delivery, land deeds and the legality of granting the foot of First Street as a ferry landing to a private party. C.M. Davis and 150 other citizens, including founder Robert Semple, petitioned the council on February 9, 1852, to resolve the problems. Their main interest was in attracting the capital to Benicia by building a city hall. The council appointed the petitioners to a special committee and told them to return with specific recommendations. A week later, the council passed a resolution "to embody therein an offer of one or two squares, being each 600 feet square as a site or sites for Capitol Building and other State Edifices. Resolved further, that the Committee be instructed to draft a memorandum on the subject to the legislature and report on same the next meeting of the Council."[84]

The proposal was solidified on February 19, 1852, when the council voted for a special resolution, which offered two squares of land to the state for a capitol site. Another resolution, passed March 19, defined the city's position further:

*His honor the Mayor be authorized to proceed to Sacramento City forthwith on behalf of Benicia in case the Legislature agrees to permanently locate*

Sketch of Benicia by James D. Hutton, circa 1849. *Courtesy Benicia Historical Museum.*

> *the Capitol at Benicia, to enter into agreement with the state to remove the*
> *Capital buildings from Vallejo in case those buildings be determined to be*
> *bonafide property of the State of California, to Benicia, and erect and*
> *furnish same in good substantial workmanship.*[85]

Added to the motion was another, which stated, "Agreed that Benicia is to furnish all necessary offices for Public Officers of the State until the public building is complete at the expense of the City of Benicia." The city had just promised to construct a building for the state.[86]

A new council chamber was created in a rented house. On June 7, the council authorized the movement of furniture, and on June 21, the council authorized the city marshal to furnish the chamber with spittoons. The need for a city hall continued to be a problem and was addressed in a memorandum from the mayor on August 2, 1852. On August 9, a motion was made to refer the matter of a city hall to committee with Dr. Peabody, the village physician, as chairman. A week later, on August 16, the council received a report that listed several plans. Being a new city on the frontier, Benicia had few empty buildings or meeting rooms. Peabody also reported that Thomas Larkin would donate any lot in his possession to the city to be used to erect a city hall. A public vote was called for August 23 to settle the issue.[87]

At the meeting on August 23, the following resolution was passed:

*Whereas, by a nearly unanimous vote of the electors of the City of Benicia held August 23, inst. AD 1852, the Council of said City were authorized to make a loan creating a special indebtedness not to exceed twenty-five thousand dollars for the purpose of erecting a city hall. Said hall to be built of brick or stone. For other improvements, the Mayor and other members of the Special Committee for erection of city hall be authorized to ascertain if a loan can be negotiated and on what turn.*[88]

The council must have had a specific plan in mind because they were exacting in their instructions for the contract bid:

Ten days authorized to advertise for proposals for building according to following specifications:
a. 45 x 80 feet dimensions, 4 feet elevation, stone foundation.
b. Lower floor in the clear, 16 feet; one room 60 x 45; 4 rooms 17 x 10, with brick partitions plastered and hard finished.
c. Thickness of walls—lower story, 16 feet; upper story 12 feet.
d. Stone caps and sills to windows.
e. Stone steps, pillars and high stone ornamental finish over door.
f. Hall 10 feet wide.
g. Power reserved to the Committee to alter the above specifications as they see fit, providing they maintain the main features proposed.

Photographic view of Benicia, circa 1900. *Courtesy Benicia Historical Museum.*

At the same time, major widening and grading of G and H Streets were authorized.[89]

At a special meeting called on August 30, 1852, a loan of $25,000 at 12 percent per annum for three years was authorized to create the city hall. The problem simmered for the next two weeks because a loan could not be negotiated with a San Francisco company, and a temporary bond sale had to be authorized. Nevertheless, plans for the hall continued, and on September 20, a call for bids was advertised. At the September 27 council meeting, the sealed bids were opened, and the San Francisco–based construction company of Rider and Houghton came in with a bid of $24,800 and was awarded the contract. Another firm, Miner and Robinson, also presented a bid, but it was more than the $25,000 budget. At that meeting, the construction bonds received final approval and the city surveyor was instructed to stake out the corners of lot twelve, block twenty with the hall facing G Street. The final resolution approved J. Franklin Houghton and L.A. Rider as the prime contractors. The final contract was approved on October 4, 1852.[90]

Over the following weeks, the deeds for the property to transfer from Thomas Larkin and Robert Semple to the city were accepted, and multiple changes were made to the original plan. The source of the design was lost until a century later. While refurbishing the building, architects realized that the city hall was constructed from plans and instructions contained in *The*

The United States military post at Benicia, circa 1850. *Courtesy Benicia Historical Museum.*

*Modern Builder's Guide* by Minard Lafever, which was published in 1846. The city and the contractors followed the book to the point that the front columns were an exact copy of the illustrations. As is typical of owner-contractor relationships then and now, the council changed the number of rooms and dimensions several times. The architects also confirmed that some timbers for the construction of the hall came from ships stranded in San Francisco Harbor during the gold rush. However, 7,616 feet of cut boards were transported by a schooner, *Dolphin*, from Redwood Landing—now Redwood City—on June 17, 1853. The stones for the hall foundation came from a quarry already in operation along the shoreline at Semple Crossing and West Second Streets. The bricks came from a company on First Street. The name of one of the original construction workers, Anthony Howe, is known from his obituary. He died in 1908 at the age of eighty.[91]

Bill of lading for the transfer of lumber to Benicia for use in the building of the capitol. *Courtesy Benicia Historical Museum.*

The intended purpose of the building was not a well-kept secret. The *Daily Alta California* on December 15, 1852, reported, "A large, fine brick edifice has been created here, intended for a city hall, but it is rumored strong effort will be made to induce the Legislature to hold its meetings within its walls."[92]

On January 3, 1853, it was reported to the council that the hall was complete—except final painting. The mayor accepted the key from Houghton and Rider in a short ceremony the next day. The project came in on time and under budget. At the same meeting, the council authorized expenditures to bring the state archives and furniture from Vallejo.[93]

At the following meeting on February 21, the committee of one hundred citizens argued their cause and the city council voted unanimously to instruct the mayor to issue a conditional deed to the state to use the hall as a state capitol. The condition was that if the state left, the property would revert to city ownership. The council also committed to paying the rents for various state agencies, including the secretary of state, who occupied an office from April 1 to June 8 for $125 a month, and other state agencies that also ran up the bill considerably. A private home was leased as the governor's residence. The lease on the current council chambers was extended as the hall was repurposed to be the capitol. However, by September there was still debate on how the title to the property would be transferred to the state.[94]

# 7
# Benicia

## The Third Capital of California

On February 11, 1853, the state archives, furniture and treasury were transferred from Vallejo to Benicia on two large scows towed by the steam-powered tugboat *Firefly*. The state treasury funds were contained in a large safe that crashed through the decks of the scow when the ropes broke. The safe landed on the beams of the hull. The assembled crew peered through the hole in the deck in amazement that the safe didn't go through the hull and sink the ship. As the *Daily Alta California* reported, "Vallejo is now left destitute and deserted." The paper also reported that the state treasurer and controller located "a couple of neat and elegant offices at a convenient distance from the Capitol in Benicia."[95]

In homes and business properties leased by the City of Benicia for use by the state, various offices popped up. The Governor's Mansion was a simple white residence rented for the purpose. The highly valued archives and state treasury were situated in a house that is still standing on East D Street. Other offices were scattered around town. Rapidly constructed boardinghouses, hotels, taverns, gambling houses, stores, barbershops, livery stables and brothels flourished on First Street. Steamboats arrived regularly from San Francisco, Stockton and Sacramento, bringing people and products to the burgeoning and busy town. The only church in operation at the time, the Presbyterian church, did a land-office business. There were only two dirt roads out of Benicia—one that meandered around hills to Vallejo and a second that paralleled the Carquinez Straits, skirted the Suisun Marsh and cut east to Sacramento.

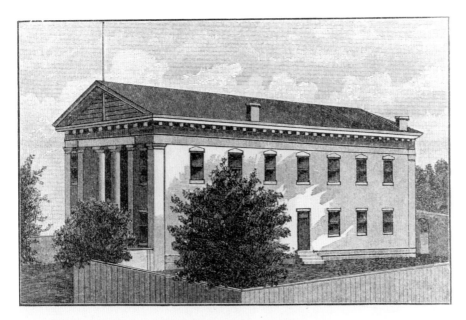

Engraved in 1888 by Charles H. Holmes of Sacramento; taken from an old photograph.

### Capitol at Benicia—1853-1854.

The Benicia State Capitol, circa 1854. *Courtesy Benicia Historical Museum.*

This house on East D Street was used as the treasury and archives while the legislature met in Benicia, 2019. *Courtesy Reg Page.*

TABLE 2: OFFICERS WHILE THE STATE GOVERNMENT WAS IN BENICIA

| Officers | Fourth legislature 1853 | Fifth legislature 1854 |
|---|---|---|
| Governor | John Bigler | John Bigler |
| Lieutenant governor | Samuel Purdy | Samuel Purdy |
| Secretary of state | W.V. Voorhies James W. Denver | James W. Denver C.H. Hempstead |
| Controller | W.S. Pierce | Samuel Bell |
| Treasurer | Richard Roman | S.A. McMeans |
| Attorney general | S.C. Hastings | J.R. McConnell |
| Surveyor general | W.M. Eddy | B.H. Marlette |
| Superintendent of public instruction | John G. Marvin | Paul K. Hubbs |
| Superintendent of public buildings | J.S. Graham | Position eliminated |
| Quartermaster general | W.H. Richardson William C. Kibbe | William C. Kibbe |
| State printer | Eugene Casserly | G. Kerr & Co. B.B. Redding |
| Translator | W.E.P. Hartnell | W.E.P. Hartnell |

*"The California State Register and Yearbook of Facts: 1859," San Francisco: Henry G. Longley and Samuel A. Morison, 1859.*

The senate met in Benicia at noon on February 11, 1853, and started with a prayer by Reverend Sylvester Woodbridge, the first minister of the first Protestant church in California, which was located in Benicia.[96] The group had a lot to do because of the time spent hauling the state capital from one city to another. The legislative year for the fourth legislature lasted from January 3, 1853, to May 19, 1853, and the fifth legislature lasted from January 2, 1854, to May 15, 1854. The legislators and executive branch quickly became engaged in continuing the organization of the new state. There were 90 legislators in the fourth session and 114 in the fifth. While the legislature and governor were in Benicia, 199 statutes were passed and signed into law—more than the previous legislatures.

TABLE 3: THE NUMBER OF LEGISLATORS WHO MET IN BENICIA

| Legislature | Year | Senate | Assembly | Totals |
|---|---|---|---|---|
| Fourth | 1853 | 27 | 63 | 90 |
| Fifth | 1854 | 34* | 80 | 114 |

*The first senate district had two members rather than the one that was provided for in the apportionment of 1853. The second member was sworn in.

*"The California State Register and Yearbook of Facts: 1859," San Francisco: Henry G. Longley and Samuel A. Morison, 1859.*

TABLE 4: STATUTES PASSED IN BENICIA

| Legislature | Year | Laws | Joint resolutions | Concurrent resolutions | Totals |
|---|---|---|---|---|---|
| Fourth | 1853 | 169 | 17 | | 186 |
| Fifth | 1854 | 9 | 1 | 3 | 13 |
| Total | | 178 | 18 | 3 | 199 |

*"The California State Register and Yearbook of Facts: 1859," San Francisco: Henry G. Longley and Samuel A. Morison, 1859.*

There was a lot to do in the areas of education, land law, prisons and professional licensing. The foundations for the University of California and a public education program for children were laid. There was debate and legislation over the wages of judges, as well as county boundaries and organization. San Quinton State Prison was also authorized.

A more detailed analysis of the statutes passed in Benicia gives the story of a new state organizing itself and the forces that were tugging at the legislature and governor:

TABLE 5: TYPES AND NUMBERS OF LAWS PASSED IN BENICIA

| Type of statute | Fourth legislature 1853 | Fifth legislature 1854 |
|---|---|---|
| Labor law | 2 | |
| State organization | 8 | 1 |

| Type of statute | Fourth legislature 1853 | Fifth legislature 1854 |
|---|---|---|
| Sale of state property | 1 | |
| Courts | 12 | 1 |
| State budget, finance and taxes | 38 | 3 |
| Duties of public officials | 18 | |
| Funding county debt | 11 | |
| Estate law | 2 | |
| Criminal law | 5 | |
| Name change of individuals | 2 | |
| Establish state offices, i.e. insane asylum, schools, pest house, library and prisons | 5 | |
| Organization of county and city governments | 17 | |
| Translators (Spanish and Chinese) | 3 | |
| Fisheries and game | 3 | |
| Establish an official state map | 1 | |
| Public health and welfare | 9 | 4 |
| Business | 4 | |
| Appointments | 6 | |
| Family law (divorces and husband and wife rights, rights of women) | 2 | |
| Corporate law | 6 | |
| Slaves | 1 | |
| Public works (highways, canals, streets, ferries, ports and wharves) | 8 | |
| Incorporate cities | 3 | |
| Settle land disputes | 2 | |

## COWS AND PIGS

Unpenned cows and pigs were a big issue in rural California, including in Benicia. There was considerable debate on this issue in both houses of the legislature. In search of food and water, the animals invaded houses and barns, carried off chickens and generally made a mess of everything—especially the roads. There were no paved roads in all of California at the time, except for perhaps a couple streets in San Francisco. Even in the Fog City, it was common for pigs to run between horses' hooves, causing catastrophic wagon accidents. Hogs wallowing in the water in the depressions of the streets made a stinking mess that horses and carriages had to maneuver around. The legislature finally sent a statute to the governor that required all cows and pigs be enclosed in fences, but this took decades to be enforced. California is a big state, and there were a lot of farmers with cows and pigs. Fences were expensive, and nobody was around to enforce the law. So, the problem lingered, and more pigs wandered into the path of carriages for years to come.[97]

## A MAP OF THE STATE

The state needed an official map. Under normal circumstances, a map would have already been drawn and the boundaries documented before consideration for statehood. In California, which did and still does everything its own way, the map wasn't done. The boundaries of the counties were in dispute, and there was a looming conflict with California's neighbors over boundaries. One of the issues in dispute was the ownership of Lake Tahoe, then—as now—a jewel in the Sierra Nevada range. Southern sympathizers, the self-proclaimed Chivs, wanted to split the state in two and create a second state to the south where slavery would be legal.

The previous legislature had authorized an extensive survey, and now it was time to act before any other state or country claimed any California land, including the all-important gold fields. On March 25, 1853, the first map was authorized to be printed. It didn't end the boundary disputes, but it was a big step toward consolidating the boundaries, which remain the same to this day. For a week, Lake Tahoe was called Lake Bigler in honor of the governor, but the old name stuck, and Bigler's humility stopped the action.[98]

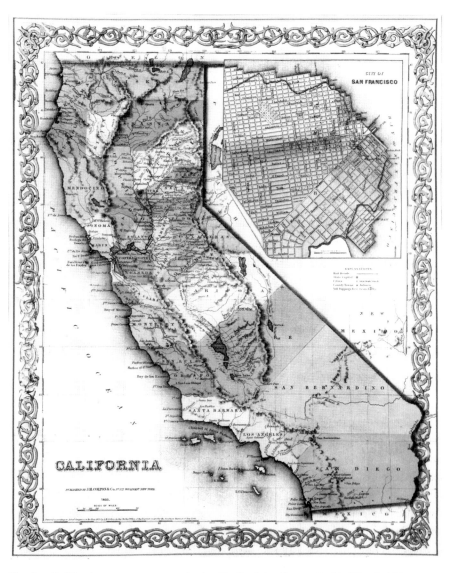

The first California state map was authorized in Benicia. *Courtesy Benicia Historical Museum.*

## Slavery and the Fugitive Slave Act

Settlers and military officers had been bringing black slaves to California from the East since the early 1840s. They worked the fields, tended to the animals and performed domestic duties. The Spanish and the Mexicans also kept slaves, mostly Indians and the descendants of Africans. When gold was discovered in 1848, slaves were brought west to work the mines. Hundreds of slaves were marched in coffles from Missouri to California to be leased out as labor. Many slave owners cut deals in which a slave would be manumitted if he spent two or three years laboring in California. It is estimated that there were about one thousand slaves in the state before emancipation in 1865.[99]

Free black men and women also went to California looking for work, as did people of mixed African and European descent. The California Constitution of 1849 outlawed slavery. The California Constitution begins with a "Declaration of Rights" that specifies twenty basic rights or classes of rights to be enjoyed by its citizens. Section eighteen states, "Neither slavery, nor involuntary servitude, unless for punishment of crimes, shall ever be tolerated in this State."[100]

Slavery was still the law of the land in the United States and had to be honored by the Full Faith and Credit clause of the Constitution. The Compromise of 1850, which allowed California to enter the Union as a free state, merely said that if a black person was born to a slave in California, he or she was free. Escaped slaves, primarily from Missouri and the South, made their way to California and were followed by bounty hunters. These were cruel and ruthless men who hunted escaped slaves for a living and often didn't bother to distinguish whether the people were free as they dragged them back to Missouri to be sold.

The first California Fugitive Slave Act was passed in 1852 by the third legislature. Titled "Respecting Fugitives from Labor, and Slaves Brought to This State Prior to Her Admission into the Union," it said, in part, "When a person held to labor in any State or Territory of the United States under the laws thereof, shall escape into this State, the person to whom such labor or service may be due, his agent or attorney, is hereby empowered to seize or arrest such fugitive from labor."[101]

The act laid out who could seize a fugitive slave, a prohibition against aiding the slave and the duties of the sheriffs in seizing them. Significantly, slaves were not able to testify on their own behalf, and it stated, "Claimants are not allowed to hold slaves in servitude in this State." In other words, the fugitive slave had to be returned to a slave state.

Free black people responded with alarm. There was little chance that they would be able to prove their free legal status because they were prohibited from testifying against white men in court. Many packed up their households and left for the Pacific Northwest, where slavery was outlawed, and there were no fugitive slave laws.[102]

The battle over slavery came with the state government to Benicia. Singleton Vaughn's slave, Adam Willis, lived not too far from the capitol. He would later be manumitted as part of a deal when he returned to the East Coast and brought Vaughn's family back to California. About thirty miles to the east of Benicia was a ranch where slaves were kept so that they could be leased out for labor in the mines. The Chivs saw the issue as a fight over property rights. They believed slaves were property to be owned, bought and sold for the benefit of their owners—it was a big and profitable business. The opponents, led by David Broadrick and Governor Bigler, saw slavery as a moral abomination. There was also opposition to slavery from an economic point of view—slaves were free competition for white miners in the gold fields. It was ugly business that eventually led to an ugly war.

In May 1853, the issue of fugitive slaves once again reached the legislature in Benicia. They voted "To amend an Act respecting Fugitives from Labor, and Slaves brought to this State, prior to her admission into the Union." Again, the act was narrow in scope and applied to fugitives who came into the state after the conquest in 1846 and before the enactment of the Monterey Constitution of 1849. It was also limited in time: "[T]he provisions of this section shall have force and effect, until the fifteenth day of April one thousand eight hundred and fifty-four, but not beyond that period."[103]

The legislature did not approve another fugitive slave law, and slavery was unequivocally outlawed by the Thirteenth Amendment to the U.S. Constitution in 1865.

## BUILDING A STATE

Many state institutions were initiated in Benicia. Prisons, the state library, an insane asylum, schools and "pest houses" for people with infections were established. Construction was authorized for highways, wharves, canals, state buildings and other capital improvements. Militias were organized and funded to hunt down and kill bandidos, and an agricultural institute was formed.

School funding occupied the first days of the legislature in Benicia. S.A. McMeans, the state treasurer, wrote that thousands of children were streaming into the state with their parents and needed to be educated. The state had to play catch-up with the education of a large number of people entering its territory and would continue to do so into the twenty-first century. There was also legislation introduced to deal with mechanics' liens, mail delivery to Calaveras County, procedure in criminal cases and the selection of the U.S. senator. On January 7, the newly elected lieutenant governor, Samuel Purdy, was sworn in by Judge Winston, of Solano County.[104]

Many of the laws passed by both sessions of the legislature in Benicia concerned businesses. After all, the business of California at the time was business. On May 30, 1853, the legislature established a standard of weights and measures. Also passed in May was the Act Defining the Rights of Husband and Wife, which gave wives—and by extension all women—the right to own property separate from their husbands. Mechanics' liens were established in May. Corporate law was initiated by the establishment of corporations and a code for their formation and operation, thus providing employment to legions of lawyers in future centuries. And contract law was codified.

## The Ladies' Groups

During both sessions, the legislature and governor were bombarded by letters and petitions from ladies' groups throughout the state. They called for an institution of the "Maine liquor laws," which is to say, Prohibition. The Maine law was passed in 1851 because of intense lobbying by temperance activists led by Neal Dow (1804–1897), a minister who campaigned intensely against alcohol. The law prohibited the sale of all alcoholic beverages except for "medicinal, mechanical or manufacturing purposes." Intense lobbying, including riots against the laws, among the working class and immigrant peoples led to its repeal in 1856. However, by 1855 twelve states were "dry." In Benicia, there was no way that the Legislature of a Thousand Drinks would vote for Prohibition, and the work in the prosperous mines of the state was fueled by liquor. The petitions from the ladies were politely accepted, and the subsequently introduced bills were tabled.[105]

## Governor Bigler is Reinaugurated

Governor John Bigler was inaugurated on January 8, 1854, in the new Benicia capitol. He had run as a Free-Soil Democrat against a large majority of proslavery Democrats from Southern California, who fashioned themselves the "Chivalry" or "Chivs." Free-Soilers argued against the spread of slavery to new states, which was too late for California. Bigler overcame Whig Party challenger William Waldo and won a second term. Nevertheless, his inaugural speech made no mention of slavery or the Chivalry. Kicking the issue of slavery down the road to eventual disaster, he talked of prosperity, industrialization and the need for schools, hospitals and roads.

When the legislature finally got to work, the issue of the state debt popped up. The state owed $3,454,815.70 in 3 and 7 percent bonds. Some $900,00 of that amount was for "war debt" and nearly $500,000 was for school warrants. The war debt was for money spent financing the California State Rangers, who mustered in on May 28, 1853. The rangers were a loosely organized group of heavily armed horsemen who chased desperados, bandidos and Indians who were harassing miners and farmers and interrupting the flow of money into the banks. Mostly, they patrolled

What may have been the governor's residence in Benicia—from the DeBenedetti papers. *Courtesy Benicia Historical Museum.*

the trails that snaked their way east from Sacramento into the gold fields. Another significant chunk of the debt was accrued in moving the capital around the state—a fact not lost on the legislators, governor, judges and staff.[106]

# THE CHINESE IMMIGRANTS

Chinese residents entered California for the same reasons as everyone else. There were intense population pressures in China that resulted in a decrease in available land and vastly unequal wealth distribution. There were also social upheavals caused by the Opium War (1839–1842) and the Taiping Rebellion (1851–1864). On the other hand, California offered opportunities for work—first in the gold mines and then on the railroads. Chinese immigrants also found work in agriculture, as factory workers and as domestics. The number of Chinese individuals in California increased from about 450 in 1850 to about 20,000 when the legislature met in Benicia.[107]

Opposition to Chinese immigration and employment fell into two overlapping groups: racists who hated the Chinese as they hated black people, Jews and everyone else; and economic opponents. Economic opposition was based on the concept that the Chinese were thought to take jobs from white workers at lower rates with longer hours. This was looked upon as unfair competition.

On the other hand, many employers and companies in California favored Chinese immigration for the same reason—the availability of cheap and hardworking labor.

The issue of immigration was a federal matter, and in Washington, D.C., there was agitation on both sides of the issue before Congress. In 1850, the California legislature passed the Foreign Miners' License Law, which imposed a tax of twenty dollars a month on all foreign miners. Many foreign miners ignored the law in the chaos of early California statehood, when the enforcement of laws was left up to county sheriffs who could be easily swayed. On the other hand, as the gold placers in the Sierra Nevada mountains began to decline in 1853 to 1854, thousands of unemployed or disenfranchised miners, including Chinese immigrants, flowed into the cities of Sacramento and San Francisco, where they formed large Chinatowns. In Benicia, the legislators discussed the issues of the Chinese ad nauseum but passed no significant laws.

## THE PECK AFFAIR

The Peck Affair splashed onto the front pages of California newspapers in late January 1853, and it stayed there for the remainder of the year. State senator Elijah Peck, from Butte County, charged that Joseph C. Palmer, a San Francisco banker, offered him $5,000 for his support of David Broderick for the United States Senate. At the time, U.S. senators were selected by state legislatures, and Broderick was especially controversial because he was a staunch abolitionist and unionist. When the accusation went to trial, Palmer reversed the situation under oath by accusing Peck of arranging a meeting during a steamer trip from Sacramento and offering his vote for $5,000.[108]

While the issue of the bribe revolved around the friendship of Palmer and Broderick and where the state capital was to be sited, the undertones of the controversary were about slavery and whether the state would continue to be controlled by the Chivs.

Attempted bribery of a member of the legislature was not against any state law at the time. "How would they otherwise eat?" went a saying of the day that applied to Congress, as well as the legislature. But it was thought to be against the rules of the state senate. At least getting caught doing it was against the rules. The attempted bribery went to a hearing in the state senate with all the trappings of a trial. Peck, at the time, was a thirty-year-old senator who worked as a miner and farmer when the legislature was not in session. He testified that Palmer offered a bribe of $5,000 if he voted to move the state government to San Francisco, and if not Fog City, then Sacramento. Palmer testified that Peck, an ally of Broderick who favored Sacramento, solicited the bribe. Several witnesses and co-conspirators testified on both sides with tales of clandestine meetings in smoke-filled bars along San Francisco's famed Barbary Coast.[109]

An editorial by the legislative correspondent in the *Sacramento Daily Union* on January 31, 1854, described the defense attorney in words that still ring true today:

> *I deem it my duty, at this time and place, as one of the spectators of the alleged bribery case, to record an emphatic protest against the manner of conducting Mr. Peck's examination. For the best portion of three days he has been kept upon the witness stand, subject to the impertinent brow-beatings, beardings, badgerings, and silly cross questionings of an opinionated third rate lawyer (from the exhibition thus far made of his legal talents, I can call his prosecutor nothing else,) who, instead of extending towards him*

*the courtesy of a dignified Senator in the midst of his compeers, takes advantage of a fortuitous privilege to magnify himself in his own estimation by playing the part of the bully towards Mr. Peak.*[110]

The hypocrisy of the affair was that many people were taking bribes of one kind or another, and nobody in the legislature wanted to advertise it. In the end, the testimony cut too close to home, and the bribery case dissolved in a whirlwind of parliamentary motions on a Friday afternoon. The members of the legislatures were able to catch the steamboats to Sacramento and San Francisco for the weekend.

# 8

# Benicia

## The Fight for a Capitol Site Continues

The deed to the Benicia City Hall had been offered to the state on February 25, 1853, and was taken up and tabled by the legislature several times. A concurrent resolution passed on March 21 accepting the deed from the mayor of Benicia to the State of California for the building and property. Ironically, in the following legislature, the governor also received a deed from the mayor of Sacramento and John Sutter for a large parcel of land known as the Public Square. A measure to return the property to Benicia was taken up in the sixth legislature on March 20, 1855, but it was tabled indefinitely on April 26 of that year.[111]

From the beginning, there was carping in the newspapers about the site of the new capital. Unsurprisingly, the *Sacramento Daily Union* had a lot to say:

> *Many of the most violent opponents of the measure at the beginning, are now willing to confess that Benicia is entirely unsuited for a permanent location. The eternal wind which keeps howling through the streets, the absence of books, society, and the general dreariness of the place, all go to make up this general opinion.*[112]

The *Sacramento Daily Union* continued the drumbeat for removal of the capital from Benicia throughout the year, citing, among other things, Benicia's "poor" weather.[113]

The *Benicia Vedette* countered with a portrayal of Sacramento as a city of sin and low morality, which was also true, but that described the entire

Executive Department
Benicia Feby 25th 1853

To,
The Senate and Assembly
of the State of California
I have the honor herewith to transmit a copy of a Deed executed on yesterday by the Mayor of the City of Benicia, which deed rests in the State of California a conditional title to the Building now occupied by the Legislature, and the lot on which it is erected.

The original Deed has been deposited in the Office of the Secretary of State, to await the decision of the Legislature on the question of its acceptance.

John Bigler

Letter of transmittal of the deed from Benicia to the California legislature. The deed was conditional on the state government remaining in Benicia. *Courtesy Benicia Historical Museum.*

state. It blasted the legislature for even thinking of moving the capital to such a town and for bending to the financial inducements the Sacramento citizenry provided.[114]

The *Sacramento Daily Union* continued the vitriol throughout the year:

> *Turning our eyes from the great metropolis of the Pacific, where shall they find a resting place? At Benicia, no! For what is Benicia? What can it*

*be? Without either position or capital, it may hope in vain for a future prosperity sufficient for the location of our California Capital. Of itself, it possesses no virtue.*[115]

The *Sacramento Daily Union* also bashed San Francisco as a den of iniquity unfit for a capital—not too far off:

*Although San Francisco would naturally present itself as the best adapted for such purposes, yet there are insuperable difficulties in the way that must forever preclude the idea. If the Capital were removed to this city, Senators and Assemblymen would soon lose their identities, and the dignity of their positions would rapidly be swallowed up and lose sight in the vortex of business, fashion, folly, dissipation, and turmoil of all kinds around them.*[116]

In February 1854, news arrived in Benicia in the *Sacramento Daily Union* of even greater gold discoveries at Mills Ranch, Badger Flat, Slate Creek, Squirrel Creek, Indian Spring, Eureka Slide and Round Tent. There was a

The *Benicia Vedette* was printed for only the period that the California state capital was in Benicia. *Courtesy Benicia Historical Museum.*

highway robbery of gold dust at Rose's Bar, which was a mining district that was more of a collection of shacks than a town in the Mother Lode region of the Sierra Nevada Mountains. The newspaper also continued the daily editorial drumbeat for removal of the capital to Sacramento.[117]

A committee to settle the capital location dispute was appointed by the legislature, comprising both senators and assemblymen. On January 13, 1854, a majority report was issued that supported Sacramento. The issue of the security of the archives was an important part of the report. At the time, the archives were housed in a private home that was rented for the state by the City of Benicia on East D Street in Benicia. The archives at the time included the records of the first five legislatures. Especially important were various documents on loans, bonds and property transactions of the young state government. Sacramento promised a substantial brick building with an ample fireproof vault.[118]

There were other issues that favored Sacramento: Benicia was too small, there was no law library (there was none in Sacramento either, but that didn't deter the committee), there was no printing plant and Benicia was connected to the rest of the state only by steamship. Sacramento, on the other hand, promised its large courthouse, extensive plots of land and a lot of monetary support. Most importantly, Sacramento was a large city with a large population that was safely inland and protected from foreign invasion. It was the hub of nine stage lines and multiple steamship lines. Multiple roads led in and out of the city, and most importantly, it was close to the all-important gold mines. Sacramento promised a large tract of land between I and J and Ninth and Tenth Streets for public buildings.

The minority report was lengthy and, in many parts, agreed with the majority concerning security of the archives and other issues. However, the committee argued that the state should remain in Benicia. They pointed out that the absence of a law library was of no consequence and that the state had already spent $93,190.54 ($23,297,500 in 2019 dollars) moving the capital around the state. It would take an additional estimated $46,472 ($11,618,000 in 2019 dollars) to move the capital to Sacramento.[119]

Into the spring, the drumbeat for removal to other towns continued. Stockton threw its hat into the ring, and San Jose and San Francisco continued to lobby for their cities. General Vallejo was silent except for quiet lobbying by his son-in-law to forgive the money that he owed the state. He eventually succeeded in lobbying the legislature and governor to pass and sign a bill to forgive the substantial debt. An editorial in the *Benicia Vedette* charged that Benicia was hampered by less than enthusiastic business support for the capital because many—if not most—of the land owners in the city were "short-sighted capitalists" in San Francisco.[120]

In February, Senator Amos Parmalee Catlin, a Chivalry Whig who represented the cities of Benicia and Vallejo, notified the senate that he would introduce a bill to move the capital to Sacramento. This was a betrayal and deep cut to Benicia. The bill was introduced, passed thirteen to eleven on February 17 and was sent to the assembly. In the assembly, there was a heated debate with representatives from Stockton, who again made a strong bid. The bill passed the assembly in a vote of thirty-nine to thirty-five on February 24 and was sent to the governor.[121]

Governor Bigler signed the bill the same day it was sent to him. He was willing to act swiftly because he had unambiguously supported Sacramento from the first day of his administration. The act read, in part, "From and after one day after the passage of this Act the permanent seat of Government of this State shall be, and the same is hereby located at the City of Sacramento, in the County of Sacramento." A joint resolution provided for adjournment to meet in Sacramento at noon on Wednesday, March 1, 1854.[122]

As to be expected, the *Sacramento Daily Union* celebrated in editorials, "The friends of Sacramento in the Legislature fought the battle gallantly and successfully."

The *San Francisco Daily Evening News* responded with sour grapes: "Your reporter feels like a cat in a strange garret." The *Alta California* reported jubilation in Sacramento.[123]

The California Supreme Court wasn't impressed. At that time, the court was meeting in San Francisco, but on March 24, 1854, the legislature required that it meet in the capital—Sacramento. The court decided on March 27 that San Jose was the legal capital. The decision was based on the court's interpretation of the Constitution of 1849, which required a two-thirds majority of both houses of the legislature for the removal of the seat of government. To add insult to injury, the justices wrote, "They had the power to select the seat of Government, but they had not power to sell the selection of it, however great may have been the pecuniary consideration." The court also noted that a plebiscite had chosen Vallejo as the capital and ended, "We have, therefore, no hesitation in declaring that the Act of February 4th, 1851 is contrary to the Constitution, and therefore invalid." In the eyes of the court, the capital was still in San Jose even though it was still a mud flat every time Coyote Creek overflowed and no improvements had been made.[124]

Nevertheless, Sacramento proceeded with a deed to the state for the promised property known as the Public Square. The issue was temporarily settled when on July 13, 1854, a massive fire destroyed most of the business district in Sacramento, including the courthouse where some of the legislative sessions of 1852 were held and where the legislature was going to meet after leaving Benicia. The *Alta California* reported that a new county courthouse was laid out in September: "The lower story intended for thieves, and the upper one for members of the Legislature." The Sacramento courthouse was deliberately laid out as a capitol for the state and was destined to be the capitol from 1855 to 1869.[125]

The legal maneuverings continued. San Jose realtors Thomas L. Vermuele and R. H. Leetch filed a request for a writ of mandamus that would order the state government to meet in San Jose. Judge Fred Appleton of the Third District Court in San Jose commanded Governor John Bigler to either perform his duties in San Jose or appear on October 28, 1854, before the District Court of Santa Clara County at San Jose. Bigler, in turn, sent the acting attorney general to court in his place to argue that the legislature did legally move the government to Sacramento and that the location of his office was where the government was located.[126]

The case went to court—before Judge Hester—at the end of October. Attorneys French and Hall represented the two real estate brokers who filed the complaint and a Mr. Stewart, the acting attorney general, and Colonel P.L. Edwards represented the state. After lengthy arguments and an even longer written decision, Judge Hester ruled for the San Jose real estate brokers and against the state.[127]

Meanwhile, the sharks were circling the Benicia state capitol. Sacramento put on a full court press to retain the capital. Benicia was running out of money both for lobbying (in other words paying bribes) and for paying for the rent of residences and offices to be used as state buildings. San Jose continued to litigate and lobby. Representatives from Stockton and San Francisco continued their efforts.

It was Governor Bigler's maneuvering that finally brought the capital to Sacramento. Justice Wells, a pro–San Jose justice, died, and Bigler appointed an ally, Charles H. Bryan, to replace him. Once sworn in, Bryan concurred with Chief Justice Murray's opinion (there were only three justices at the time) and reversed the lower court's decision. As if to add emphasis, the court adjourned to meet in Sacramento on the first Monday of February in 1855.[128]

The legislature officially decamped for Sacramento and traveled by barge to its new location. The state government has remained in

The current California state capitol in hot, humid, foggy Sacramento, circa 1920. *Courtesy Benicia Historical Museum.*

Sacramento since and has gone through several building programs and remodels. The politics of where to place the seat of government continued until an enormous amount of money was spent for a large, permanent capitol, which was built between 1861 and 1874. It was built as if to say, "We're here to stay."

# 9
# Benicia

## The State Decamps

After the move to Sacramento, the Benicia City Hall sat empty. Also missing was the $19,000 a year fee that the government was paying the city for use of the state buildings. To make matters worse, the city had a long-term lease on a facility to use as council chambers. At the council meeting on March 6, 1854, the committee in charge of moving the capital from Vallejo to Benicia was asked to present a report on what went wrong. A plan was formulated to lease a portion of the hall to the County of Solano.

## THE CITY HALL BECOMES THE COUNTY SEAT

Within the month, the lower floor of the hall was leased to the County of Solano for $1,500 per year—enough to make payments on the construction loan. Benicia remained the county seat for two decades, until more money changed hands and the county decamped for Fairfield. By having the county government in Benicia, the city population stabilized. It could be true that the number of government workers living in Benicia and working for Solano County was greater than the number working for the state. The county courts were also located in Benicia—all crowded into the city hall and a few surrounding buildings on First Street.

At the meeting on March 20, Reverend William Wilmott asked if the hall could be used for religious purposes. The request was granted. However, the title of the property was in question, and on May 30 the city attorney was directed to do a search. There was no apparent chain of title from the Mexican government to Vallejo and from Vallejo to Larkin and from Larkin to the city.[129]

At the council meeting on September 11, the clerk was directed to move all papers, books and furniture to the second floor of the city hall. At the following meeting, the purchase of chairs and other furniture for the city offices was authorized. The back rent on the former city offices was paid off. The carpet cost $15.55 and the chairs cost $54, and it was all carefully detailed in account books that still survive in the city archives.[130]

## THE CITY LOSES THE HALL TO FORECLOSURE

There were problems with the payments the city was supposed to be making. The city was late in payments on the construction loan, so the lending company of Hall and Cooke, Owen, Baxter and Company placed a lien on the property. On the other hand, Cook and Owen probably would not have issued the loan if there had been no clear title and a clause that the property would revert to city ownership if the state stopped using it. The title from the city to the state was probably never filed. Lawyers scurried to the document books and files, and the bill was $85.50. During the following week, a settlement was achieved:

> *Cook and Owen will settle the amount of their claim, at about $7000, payable out of license revenue in cash, as same may be collected within fifteen months from the date of purchase, bearing 2% monthly interest. The monies arising from the lease of building also to be applied to the purchase of Hall by the City.*[131]

To increase revenue in order to pay off the debts, the city started to rent out the second story of the hall. F. Denison was authorized to use it for religious services on Thursday evenings, another church used it on Sundays and L. Leslie used it for an exhibition.

The deal with Cook and Owen didn't work out—probably because the city was unable to guarantee payment. At a special meeting of the council, the following resolution was passed:

*Whereas, Mrs. Cooks and Owen, having purchased the City Hall under execution v. City of Benicia and time of redemption having expired, they, having obtained a deed from the Sheriff of Solano County, and being the owners thereof, said Cooks and Owen having demanded possession of said premises,*

*Be It there resolved: The City Clerk is directed to surrender to Cooks and Owen or agent the keys to the City Hall.*

At the same meeting, the council ordered the city government to vacate and to notify the controller of Solano County that the office of Cook and Owen was to receive their rent payments.[132]

The city council continued to look for a resolution of their financial situation and for a new place to meet. One idea that was floated, and eventually implemented, was to rent the upper floor of the hall from Owens and Cook for one dollar. Another was to sue the State of California for nonfulfillment of the agreement to move the capital to Benicia. Nevertheless, the council continued to sublet the upper floor as if nothing had happened. The council decided to sell its own bonds and purchased a plate, paper, ink and a press to do so. The problem was that the council had been authorizing and printing bonds for three years and a lot were out there, including some that had never been authorized. The "bad paper" destroyed the creditability of the bonds and eliminated any credit the city might try to establish.[133]

As can be expected, the issue of the city hall disintegrated into litigation, and the council hired lawyers to settle the issue of the title once and for all. Attorney Harry Lee was retained at a fee of $1,000 to represent the city in a lawsuit against Cook and Owen.

The debacle of the capital in Benicia came back to haunt the council in June 1855, when the case of *Thomasina Terini v. City of Benicia* was decided against the city. As part of the deal to attract the state government to Benicia, the city agreed to pay rent for all the state offices while the legislature met there. The city promised to rent the still-standing red brick house of Terini (or Perinas) on East E Street for use by the state as the archives and treasury. While the state was there, the city paid the rent, but when the state left, the money stopped, and Terini claimed the city still owed money. The city countered by saying that the backstabbing state government was responsible for the rent after the first month. There was obviously more than a little bitterness in Benicia at the time. The superior court said otherwise, and the city had to pay $300 and legal fees.[134]

Into the fall of 1855, city council attorneys met in secret with Cox and Owens to hammer out a deal away from all the competing business interests that had some kind of a claim against the city. The council continued to meet on the upper floor of the hall, and the city offices continued to be sublet to churches and other groups. All rents, including those paid by the County of Solano to use the hall as the county seat, went to Cox and Owens.[135]

A deal was made. In November, S.C. Hastings, a former state attorney general, purchased the entire property and deeded the half of the property that the city hall was on back to the city. The city attorney presented the deed to the city council on November 12 without fanfare. The city had its hall back but had to part with some of the property where the Fischer-Hanlon House is now located. Over several months, S.C. Hastings also received the deeds to several underwater lots. Nevertheless, the city still had to pay off the bonds that had been used to pay off the Cox and Owens debt.[136]

The new year brought some movement on the hall. In February, the council started payments on the debt again. After the death of Semple in 1854, and when the state legislature ceded the waterfront to the city, the city discovered that it owned the underwater lots in the city and started to sell them. They made a considerable amount of money. The underwater lots were used as areas to be filled for commercial uses, to be covered with wharves and as mooring for ships and houseboats called arks. The issue of the authorized and unauthorized bonds was resolved. The city also won a lawsuit with the water company and profited by $1,000. The tax collection system was stabilized.

## THE FIRE DEPARTMENT COMES TO THE HALL

A volunteer fire department was formed on February 4, 1856, after a hotel partially burned on First Street. The names of the first volunteers are lost to history, but they were given use of a room in the second level of the hall for their organizational materials and some equipment. A fire bell, which was cast at the Pacific Mail Works in Benicia, was placed on top of the city hall to alert the populace and summon the volunteers in the event of a fire. The first fire engine, which is still in a city museum, had been purchased used from a fire department on the East Coast for $1,500 the previous fall and shipped around the Horn. The first firehouse was established in a barn leased in May for $97 a month. In October of that year, the city enlarged the house for a cost of $200.[137]

## THE HALL BECOMES A COURTHOUSE

The Cook and Owen question still loomed over the city in 1857. The city was paying only the interest on the bonds, and a special committee was working in secret to come to a resolution. The city owned the hall again, but the rent was still going to Cook and Owen. In September, a deal was worked out. The city sold several lots, including some underwater parcels, and used some of the cash to pay off Cooks and Owens. The remainder of the funds paid for transfer and attorneys' fees. At the same time, Judge Curry and Judge Hastings set up court in a room in the upstairs area, and the rents were used for building maintenance. Hastings and Curry would later propose to buy the building but were rebuffed.[138]

## THE SCHOOL BOARD COMES TO THE HALL AND THE CITY RECORDS ARE HELD HOSTAGE

Despite the loss of the state government, the population of Benicia slowly grew as agriculture and small manufacturing increased in the city. In the fall of 1858, the city council organized the Benicia Board of Education—a task it had previously filled. A room in the city hall was set aside for the board and its one secretary. The actual school was planned to be constructed two blocks away on land donated by Thomas Larkin. S.C. Hastings pointed out that part of the deal with the city was to use the hall as a school. The decision was delayed while the former city marshal held the city records hostage for money he said was owed to him for overtime and other tasks. The marshal simply loaded all of the city documents and record books into a buckboard and transported them to a hidden location. The issue was disputed, and of course, the city attorney was consulted. However, when the city paid the ransom and received the files, it discovered that Hastings was right. As the school construction slowly progressed in 1859, the upper story of the hall was turned over to the Benicia School Board for classes.[139]

Schoolchildren and adults in front of the Benicia City Hall, circa 1856. *Courtesy Benicia Historical Museum.*

## THE CIVIL WAR YEARS

During the Civil War, the city was left with a building too large for its needs and too large for it to maintain—especially after the school board moved into new quarters and the school construction was completed. Further, the County of Solano had decamped for Fairfield. In February 1861, the council proposed to the state legislature that it would gratuitously surrender the building for use as a state reform school, normal school, state university

Members of the California Volunteers during the Civil War, circa 1864. *Courtesy Benicia Historical Museum.*

or other institute. The legislature deferred the offer, undoubtably distracted by the war. However, the Benicia Garfield Guards, or Benicia Rifles as it was called—an antislavery, anti-secession militia unit organized by T.G. McDonald—was allowed to use the hall as an armory for thirty dollars a month. There was a significant group of secessionists in Benicia at the time, despite the presence of the Benicia Arsenal, which was clearly in Union control. The Benicia Rifles was a privately financed group armed by the U.S. Army out of the Arsenal. The Rifles drilled regularly but didn't deploy anywhere else in the state. They continued to drill and rent the hall as an armory for two years.

The California Volunteers was another organization altogether. The Volunteers was a regular army unit based in the Presidio of San Francisco and used the post scrip "C.V." to distinguish itself from the units on the East Coast. It was composed of three regiments of cavalry, six regiments of infantry, one battalion of mountaineers and one battalion of Native Cavalry that was headed by Colonel Reynaldo Pacheco, who later became governor. Patrolling the fourteen western states, the California Volunteers, and various pro-Union militias, kept these secessionists in check during the war. All of the volunteer units and many of the militia units came through the Benicia Arsenal for equipment and munitions, and many of them spent time visiting the bars and brothels of First Street in Benicia.[140]

# THE LAND TITLE IS CLEARED

The Rancho Suscol case finally settled the issue of the property ownership. The U.S. Supreme Court decided against General Vallejo, leaving the land that was once Rancho Suscol (and Benicia) to the federal government. On

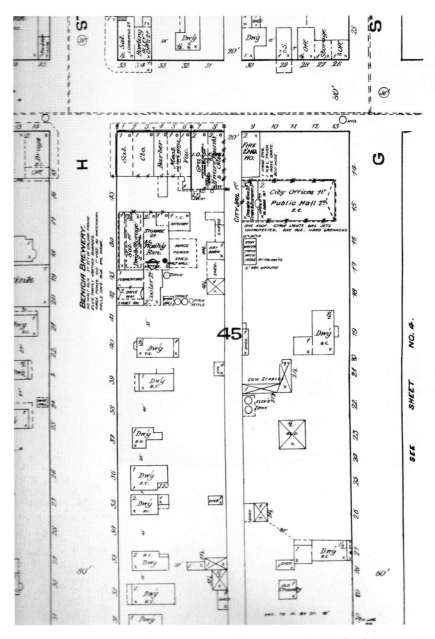

A cropped portion of the 1886 Sanborn map of Benicia showing details of the extension and the firehouse. *Courtesy Benicia Historical Museum.*

July 23, 1866, Congress passed the Benicia Townsite Grant, which allowed property owners within the townsite to request patents from the federal government. That year, the city received a patent signed by President Andrew Johnson that ceded the land where the hall was located to the city.

## More Construction to and around the Hall

While the records are lost and the exact date of the construction of a fire station is unclear, an 1885 Sanborn map clearly shows that a side structure, not connected to the city hall, was present. It was used as a fire station for many years, until it was finally torn down during the 1958 reconstruction. Inscriptions on the map document that the fire station had one hand engine, one hook and ladder truck, two hose carts and eight hundred feet of hose.

Washing the steps of the old capitol on Admission Day, circa 1955. Pictured in this yearly ceremony is the original fire engine purchased in 1855 and the fire chief, Jerry Dana. *Courtesy Benicia Historical Museum.*

Photo showing the capitol building and the extension at the rear. Note the fire escape added in the early twentieth century, circa 1950. *Courtesy Benicia Historical Museum.*

The Benicia City Hall with the firehouse in the foreground, capitol building in background and the fire bell on top of the rear extension of the building, circa 1900. *Courtesy Benicia Historical Museum.*

Behind the fire station there was an extension to the original building, which was used as a jail on the ground floor and dressing rooms and stage scenery storage on the second floor. At the time, there was a public hall with a stage on the second floor that was connected to the storage room by a door where a window is now located. The stage lights were lit by unprotected gas jets, and "hand grenade" fire extinguishers were present in case of fire. There was also a cast-iron water tank with a hose on the grounds for firefighting.

# Benicia

## The Native Sons Intervene

T he post–World Wars period saw a tremendous surge in civic pride and responsibility. The city had survived two wars and a serious influenza epidemic. It was time to look to the future. In stepped the Native Sons of the Golden West, who were in the process of celebrating the centennial of the founding of Benicia. A member, Stephen DeBenedetti, set off a sequence of events that resulted in the current Benicia Capitol State Park.

## WORLD WAR I

World War I may have been fought in Europe, but Benicia was deeply engaged. The United States Arsenal geared up to provide all of the weapons and equipment for a complete infantry division and then shipped tons of material to supply it. The swine flu epidemic swept through the city, killing six of its citizens and leaving hundreds more seriously ill. Churches sponsored bandage rolling meetings.[141]

The Benicia City Hall became a focus of patriotic parades and recruitment drives. In the 1880s, the top floor had become a theater where plays and lectures were staged. The top level of the extension was used to store props. During the war, various patriotic lectures and plays were presented. The city council and government continued to operate out of the first floor. A private water company provided water to the city, and a private electric company served the hall and the surrounding blocks. The jail in the first level of the extension was used for a rotating cast of miscreants, who were presented to the justice court that also met on the first floor.

Sometime in the 1930s, the theater was discontinued because motion picture theaters provided more entertainment. The second story was largely left to the birds—literally—and a cramped library continued to function in the first story. As the Depression settled in, less money was available for repairs to the hall, and the top floor was left to disintegrate.

# WORLD WAR II

The Second World War was not easy for Benicia. On December 7, 1941, when word of the Pearl Harbor raid reached the Benicia Arsenal, more than one hundred convoys of trucks left the grounds with arms and munitions for army installations along the California coast. It was cold that day, and a blanket of thick fog covered the Arsenal and muffled the sounds as truck after truck was loaded until there was literally nothing left. No one was in a mood to talk; there was suddenly a war, and a job had to be done. A stunned, purposeful silence descended on the Arsenal and Benicia. When one installation called for more weapons, the Arsenal cabled back that it had sent out all it had. The installation sent back a message stating, "Send us your brooms and we'll beat them to death."[142]

Yuba Manufacturing Company, a large steel processing facility a mile east of the city hall, went into high gear making equipment for the war. The clang of its machines could be heard throughout the town, and everyone set their daily schedules around the company whistle. The high school ran classes in the early morning so that the students could work in the Arsenal, fields or manufacturing plants in the afternoon.

Men and women streamed into the town to work in the Arsenal, tanneries, packinghouses, lumberyards and Yuba Manufacturing, which made more than half of the howitzers used by the United States in the war. Temporary buildings popped up in the Arsenal and around the town as more and more people arrived. The churches opened around-the-clock childcare centers for the thousands of women who joined the workforce. Downtown, two motion picture theaters and about forty-five brothels, gambling dens and bars provided nonstop entertainment.

U.S. Army photo of the Benicia Arsenal during World War II, 1944. *Courtesy Benicia Historical Museum.*

The hall became the center of the United Service Organization (USO), which held dances at least twice a week. The library had extended hours. The city council continued to meet, but most of the city employees were off fighting the war, and there were no supplies to do any maintenance to speak of. So, the hall fell into even greater disrepair. Italian prisoners of war did most of the civil work, including building sidewalks that exist to this day.

On July 17, 1944, the Port Chicago Navy Magazine on the south bank of the Carquinez Straits near Benicia exploded. While 380 military people were killed and 320 were wounded, hundreds of Benicians were injured when virtually all of the windows in the city were destroyed by a massive blast radiating from the depot. Along with all of the windows on First Street, all of the windows in the hall were blown out, and glass shards flew into the houses around it. Hundreds of Benicians suffered superficial wounds from flying glass that night. An emergency Red Cross hospital already positioned in Benicia opened at St. Dominic's Church, and physicians were up all night suturing wounds. Later, the navy would pay the cities, churches and other

# DEATH TOLL RISES TO 322 IN NAVY BLAST; 500 HURT

## San Francisco Examiner

**FINAL**

VOL. CLXXXI. NO. 19 ★ ★ ★ SAN FRANCISCO, WEDNESDAY, JULY 19, 1944 DAILY 5 CENTS. SUNDAY 15 CENTS

### Death Toll Rises to 322 in Blast; Only Four Bodies Found

*Hundreds of Shells Hunted After 2 Ships Blow Up At Port Chicago*

Naval authorities announced late yesterday that the toll of dead from the explosion of two ammunition freighters at Port Chicago had risen to 322 men and possibly will reach 372.

In addition, the Nation's worst wartime disaster injured approximately 500 men, women and children, of whom an estimated 200 were military personnel. About fifty of these were injured seriously.

Only four bodies had been found, and Navy officers said they expect to find few if any more.

All others simply disintegrated in the vortex of an explosive force so tremendous that heavy steel deck plates turned white hot and shredded into shrapnel.

**Unexploded Ammunition Sought**

*Above*: Newspaper headline on the Port Chicago Explosion, 1944. *Courtesy Benicia Historical Museum.*

*Left*: Claim for damages to the city hall from the Port Chicago Explosion. *Courtesy Benicia Historical Museum.*

The Benicia City Hall (old state capitol) from the First Street side showing the entrance to the library, and to the right, the Benicia fire department, circa 1948. The fire bell is on top of the roof of the extension. Notice the fountain and trough to the right. *Courtesy Benicia Historical Museum.*

property owners for repairs, but scars can be seen today. The stained glass "Good Shephard" window and the "Jesus Window" at the Community Congregation Church on West Second Street bear cracks and other damage from the explosion.

Benicia was in flux in the years following the war—people were returning from war, war dead were being buried, people were leaving to return to other jobs or school and people were recovering from the grief of losing their loved ones. It was also the centennial celebration of Robert Semple's founding of Benicia.

## THE NATIVE SONS

On the night of September 18, 1947, Stephen DeBenedetti stood at a meeting of the Benicia Parlor of the Native Sons of the Golden West and proposed that the old state capitol should be turned over to the state as a historical monument. His fellow members greeted the suggestion with enthusiasm and appointed him as chairman of the committee to take the necessary legal and political steps to implement the proposal.[143]

By the mid-twentieth century, the old state capitol had fallen into disrepair, circa 1950.
*Courtesy Benicia Historical Museum.*

A committee was formed; it included Leland Fisher, Hartley Russell, Urban Briato and Frank Passalacqua, with DeBenedetti as chair. They met with the Benicia mayor and city council, who enthusiastically embraced the idea, given the fact that the city hall was too small for their use and was partially shared with the library. The second floor was completely unusable, and nobody really wanted to venture up the stairs. The committee met with state senator Joseph R. Knowland and Governor Earl Warren. Knowland, himself a prominent Native Son and chairman of the State Monument Committee for half a century, was enthusiastic about the proposal. As chairman of the State Park Commission, he was able to move the issue. Governor Warren was also in favor of the proposal and committed to signing any bill that came before him concerning the building.[144]

The Native Sons also formed the Benicia State Capital Restoration Inc., which was composed of members, the governor, members of the legislature and the commanding officer of the Arsenal, to lobby the legislature and Parks Department for restoration of the capitol.

The committee met with state senator Luther Gibson of Vallejo and Assemblyman Ernest Crowley and asked them to introduce a bill in the

Members of the Native Sons Capitol Committee, *front row, left to right*: Hartley Russell, Urban Braito, Luther Gibson, Gordon Kishbaugh, Orville Johnson, *back row, left to right*: Leland Fisher, Frank Pasalacqua, Steven DeBenedetti, Thomas Levy, Raymond Duvall and E.W. Prouty, 1957. *Courtesy Benicia Historical Museum.*

legislature to restore the structure. The bill passed the legislature and was signed by Governor Earl Warren on August 4, 1949. Events clicked fairly rapidly following the signature of the governor. On February 15, 1950, the city deeded the property to the state. It then took several months to settle the property title, and on April 22, 1950, the State Parks Commission approved the acquisition. The state director of finance accepted the building on behalf of the state on January 16, 1951. The city received a sum of $75,000 and the use of the building for $1 a year until the state was ready to begin reconstruction. Something along the way slipped because the state never recorded the deed with the Solano County Recorder's Office.[145]

Nothing happened. The Korean War resulted in a lot of state, county and city staff being called back to active duty, and the money was rerouted to critical road construction to support the remobilization. Nevertheless, the Native Sons continued lobbying the legislature and governor to begin the restoration. In the meantime, the city began looking for another location for a city hall, jail and library. Finally, in 1953 the legislature appropriated $180,000 for the restoration, but the appropriation expired before funds from the tideland oil royalties became available.

Firetruck outside the city hall and fire station, circa 1950. *Courtesy Benicia Historical Museum.*

Two more years passed without action from the legislature. The Native Sons continued to lobby for the monument. In February 1955, the State Division of Beaches and Parks requested a supplemental budget of $250,000 for the restoration, which had increased due to labor and material costs. The Native Sons appeared before the legislature to support the budget request. It passed and was signed into law by the governor on July 1. The division then proceeded with the restoration, which began with thorough research of the history of the building and a careful architectural survey.

## Benicia: The City Hall is Unsafe

At the meeting on Friday, April 7, 1955, Mayor Thomas Wright informed the city council that the city hall was unsafe, and that the council needed to find other premises. In a letter from Newton B. Drury, chief of the State Division of Beaches and Parks, the state condemned the use of the building for any purpose. The building was described as "unsafe for occupancy in its present condition." It went on to say, "There may be buildings in as poor structural shape as this building, but in my experience, I have seen no worse."[146]

After being evicted by the state from the old capitol building, the Benicia City Council moved the city hall to this former bank building on First Street in 1956. The building is now called the Bohn Building after the former city attorney, John Bohn, and houses a restaurant and offices. *Courtesy Benicia Historical Museum.*

Drury's letter contained a report from Frank Johnson, a structural engineer from the State Division of Architecture, that said in part, "There are so many major defects which have been pointed out in previous reports that I shall not bring them out in detail here. However, suffice it to say that the brickwork composing the walls is so outstanding below the standard for safe construct that it is probably a major defect."

In short, between the rotting boards, disintegrating masonry and mounds of bird droppings on the upper floor, the building was a health and safety disaster. The city decamped to Wink's Tavern until new rooms in a building on First Street were ready.

The library in the old capitol was closed, and a new city library was constructed at 144 East G Street and opened on May 20, 1956. The ceremony was attended by the state and Solano County librarians and members of early Benicia families, including the granddaughter of Benicia and General Vallejo.[147]

The city council drifted from one meeting place to another until 1961, when it purchased the Benicia High School complex, which was left empty when the school moved to its current quarters on Military Avenue. The building was originally constructed in 1926 and the gymnasium in 1954. It needed substantial renovations before the city government, including the police department, occupied it.[148]

# Benicia

## The Capitol Building Restoration

Restoration of the old state capitol site began in May 1956. While the library had been moved out, the police department and city council still occupied the building. At its next meeting, the council adjourned temporarily to Wink's Tavern, an appropriate place as most of the business of the city was done there anyway.[149]

There were two major issues that Alfred Eichler, the supervising architect from the Division of Architecture of the State Department of Public Works, had to deal with: safety and "genuineness," or authenticity.

State safety experts insisted on proper scaffolding and shoring of floor and wall structures. Multiple layers of paint had to be carefully removed and analyzed for their content and historical use. While there was no asbestos in the building, the literal tons of bird droppings had to be carefully shoveled out to prevent inhalation.[150]

Eichler wrote that "genuineness" of the work was a prime essential: "There is always a strong tendency in working on such projects towards 'make believe.' True restoration work, however, requires subordination of individual imagination to exactness of design, determined through scholarly research and tangible, on-the-job, evidence."

The source of information was threefold: (1) printed and pictorial records found in libraries and archives, (2) reports of old-time residents of Benicia who were able to give firsthand accounts or data handed down from previous generations and (3) actual evidence discovered on the building exterior and within the building frame during the progress of the work.

Members of the Benicia Parlor of the Native and state officials viewing a scrapbook found in the old capitol during restoration. *front row, left to right*: Orval Johnson, construction supervisor; Steve Benedetti, chairman of the Native Sons historical committee; Ernie Gallardo; Gordon Kishbaugh, district superintendent of the State Division of Beaches and Parks; and William Davena. *Second row, left to right*: Urban Braito, president of the parlor; Dr. Aubrey Keasham, historian for the Division of Beaches and Parks; Edward Farley; Edward Prouty; Judge Hartley Russel; and J.J. Knight of the Division of Beaches and Parks. *Benicia Herald*, September 21, 1956. *Courtesy of the Benicia Historical Museum.*

Research disclosed that during the previous one hundred years, multiple alterations, additions and repairs had been made to the building. The state architects traced the design of the capitol to Minard Lafever's *The Modern Builder's Guide*. This was the simplest way to transmit the ancient concept of a Greek temple to the American frontier landscape.[151]

The exterior brick walls were constructed of underburned brick called "salmon brick." During restoration, the walls were reinforced from the inside by chiseling channels in the brick and installing steel-reinforced concrete to bring its seismic resistance up to the codes of the day. The foundations were also backed and underpinned with reinforced concrete. A layer of exterior plaster was removed from the stone foundations, thus exposing the original sandstone blocks.

The system of steel-reinforced concrete wall and foundation supports transferred the load from the weakened brick walls. The method for doing this was developed by the assistant state architect, P.T. Poage, and Orval B. Johnson, who first used it while restoring the Wells-Fargo Building at Columbia in Tuolumne County.

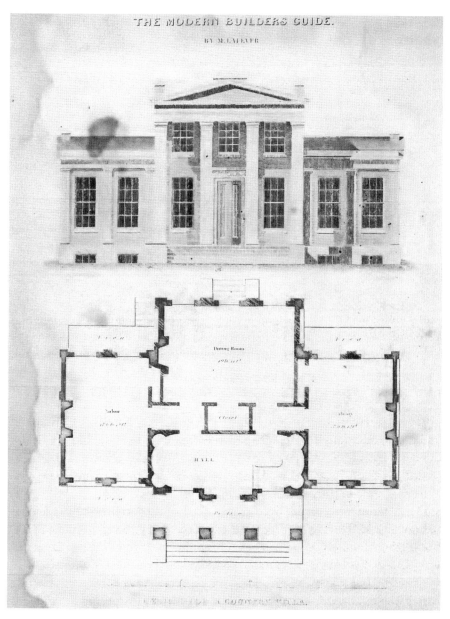

The title page from *The Modern Builder's Guide* by Minard Lafever. *Courtesy Benicia Historical Museum.*

*Above*: Scaffolding around the capitol building during restoration, 1957. *Courtesy Benicia Historical Museum.*

*Left*: The system of reinforced concrete beams inserted into the brickwork, 1957. *Courtesy Benicia Historical Museum.*

Timbers and safety shoring during restoration, 1956. *Courtesy Benicia Historical Museum.*

The roof was completely reconstructed, including the trusses. Review of period photographs suggested the original roof was tin. The state architects' research revealed the roof was made of sheet-iron plates coated with a mixture of lead and tin. This product, called "terne plate," originally came from Wales. The roof was replaced with similar plates.

The floor joists were original and hand cut. They were retained, as were the interior wood columns, which were made from used, hand-shaped masts taken from ships abandoned in San Francisco Harbor during the gold rush. Random-width floorboards made of knotty pine were discovered after several layers of linoleum were removed. The boards had been laid

Close-up of the reinforcing rods and concrete beam placement in the brick walls, 1957. *Courtesy Benicia Historical Museum.*

over fifty-foot-long fir and redwood timbers—the same ones brought from Redwood City in 1853. The floor layout was restored to that of 1853. Nail holes in the floor and the lathing behind the plaster revealed the original placement of walls and stairs. The doors and windows were restored with authentically designed reproductions. Ponderosa pine, the same wood used in 1853, was used on the entry porch and steps.[152]

The extension in the back of the building that housed the jail, the dressing rooms and storage for a stage was demolished, which restored it to its original floor plan.

Demolition of the brick and stone extension to the capitol building, 1957. *Courtesy Benicia Historical Museum.*

Plaster marks on the walls showed the locations of partitions and even a boarded-up stair. The doors, long-since bricked over, were located by identifying sandstone sills and wooden headers. The entry door was found to have been of greater dimensions than the one used when the city met there. When the plaster was chipped off, the doors were found to be sixty-one inches wide and ten feet tall.

The hardware consisted of period items salvaged from other buildings in the state. The original front door lock was donated by Mrs. Constance Kambish, and the key to the lock was donated by Mrs. Carl Gutfeld. The original iron hitching post, which was manufactured in San Francisco around 1852, was donated to the state by Homer Price of Benicia. The plumbing facilities were kept outdoors, as in the original. The lighting fixtures included several mid-century oil lamps, which were procured by

STRENGTHENING— Reinforcing steel and concrete play a major role in preserving California's oldest state capitol. The 104-year-old building should withstand the ravages of nature at least another 200 years, according to Project Superintendent Orvel Johnson, because of its being firmly buttressed with the strengthening materials. Above, Albert D. Flandi is shown preparing to frame a pilaster, or column, on the second floor of the building. Reinforcing rods are shown in the column well.

Demonstration of the method of carving grooves into the brick walls and installing reinforced concrete supports, 1956. *Courtesy Benicia Historical Museum.*

The original lock on the front door was restored to the building in 1958. *Courtesy Reg Page.*

The rotten floor boards were replaced with lumber from Ponderosa pine—the same wood used in 1853. *Courtesy Reg Page.*

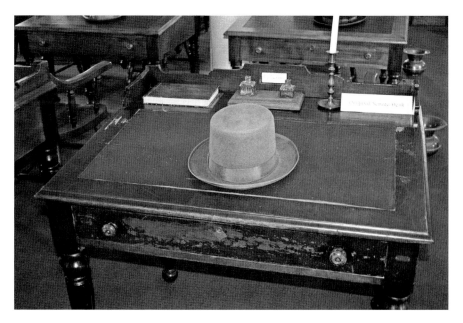

One of four tables found in a warehouse in Sacramento, thought to be from the original legislature when it met in Benicia. *Courtesy Reg Page.*

This table, and the tables like it, were manufactured in a state shop in Sonoma. *Courtesy Reg Page.*

State architects scoured the antique emporiums of the West looking for period pieces such as this one. *Courtesy Reg Page.*

The Native Sons State Capitol Committee during the reconstruction, 1957. *Courtesy Benicia Historical Museum.*

the state and wired with electricity. The elaborate fixtures in the legislature chambers were designed and manufactured by the Division of Architecture from contemporary documents. Iron stoves were donated by the Southern Pacific Railroad Company.[153]

The original plaster used sheep wool as a binder, but modern plaster mixtures were used in the reconstruction. Paint colors were reproduced after careful analysis of the original paint layers. Dark cream was daubed over white, white over gray, gray over green and green over the original light tan. The Doric columns had been painted with the same type of white paint that was used in 1853. The architects also found that the upper floor, which was used by the assembly, had a committee room on each side of the hallway and a flat ceiling instead of the open, curved ceiling that appeared in later years. The restoration was complete in July 1957, but there was no furniture. That came later.[154]

The desks, chairs and other furniture took more time. It wasn't until February 1958 that they were finally installed. They were built by the Beaches and Parks carpenter force at Sonoma and were based on models of the period, which were found in the basement of a building in Sacramento. While the original desks were made of pine with a veneer, the reproductions were made of Philippine mahogany with pine legs. The chairs included eighty-eight authentic captain's chairs made by a Sacramento firm to state specifications, twenty-four Sturbridge Windsor chairs, twelve cane ladder-back chairs, two bar stools and three deacon's benches. Clerk's tables and gallery benches were also made in the Sonoma service yard.[155]

# Benicia

## Celebration

I t was time to celebrate again. On Saturday, March 15, 1958, Governor Goodwin J. Knight and his glamorous wife, Virginia, joined members of the California senate and assembly at the opening ceremony. Special attention was given to Stephen DeBenedetti and the members of the Native Sons, who initiated the process. State senator Luther Gibson, who would later take a key role in converting the Benicia Arsenal into an industrial park, was there. The assembly held a special—and short—session to commemorate the event. Everyone wore 1850s period costumes.[156]

After the ceremony, everyone departed for a dedication luncheon held at the historic clocktower warehouse in the Benicia Arsenal. Reverend Charles Huddleston of the Benicia Congregational Church gave the benediction and Governor Knight gave a speech. The architects, engineers and officials from the state who participated in the project were also given special recognition.[157]

The old state capitol quickly became a tourist attraction. Two years after it opened, the building became a state historical monument and survived an earthquake with only minimal damage.[158]

The Benicia Capitol State Historic Park building became part of the California State Parks System. The system flourished until the 1990s, when the state legislature and governor overextended the budget due to increased spending on education and prisons.

*Above*: Leo Carrillo, Mrs. Knight, Governor Knight and Steve DeBenedetti announcing the opening of the new state park, 1958. *Courtesy Benicia Historical Museum.*

*Opposite, top*: Photo taken at the dedication of the Benicia Capitol State Historic Park, 1958. (*left to right*) Governor Goodwin J. Knight, Mrs. Virginia Knight and actor Leo Carrillo—a nephew of Benicia Vallejo. *Courtesy Benicia Historical Museum.*

*Opposite, bottom*: People assemble in period clothes for the rededication of the capitol, 1958. *Courtesy Benicia Historical Museum.*

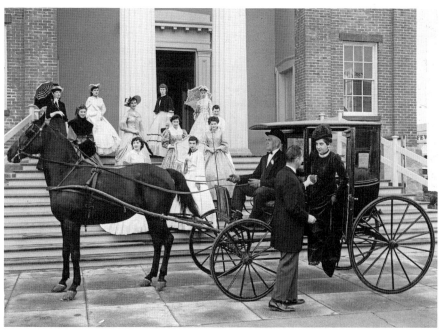

Actor Leo Carrillo, a nephew of Benicia Vallejo, at the head of the line at the celebratory ball for the restoration, 1958. *Courtesy Benicia Historical Museum.*

Edgar Strouse, the California state parks ranger at the Old State Capitol State Park, speaks to visitors, circa 1960. *Courtesy Benicia Historical Museum.*

## Return our Capital

An oval pin-on button from one of the "Return our Capitol" events, 1973. *Courtesy Benicia Historical Museum.*

Several times in the twentieth century, Benicians rallied—half in jest—to bring the capital back to their city. In 1983, about 300 Benicians rallied by yacht to Sacramento to protest in front of the "pretender" state capitol, as they termed it. The *Vacaville Reporter* printed an article that stated, "Some 300 folks from Benicia led by city officials, business leaders and even some state lawmakers launched a nautical invasion on Sacramento Saturday." Sacramento boosters responded, "The mini-war is a tongue-in-cheek affair, of course, ostensibly designed to promote Benicia as a prime resort town and better its image still tarnished by a long history as the state capital of brothels." Low blow.[159]

## The Legislature Returns, If Only for a Day

In 2000, to celebrate the 150th anniversary of the founding of the state, the state assembly and senate reconvened in the old capitol. Fire stairs and other much-needed upgrades were installed just before the meeting. The *Benicia Herald* wrote,

> *Rain pummeled the copper-sheathed roof of California's Benicia State Capitol yesterday as Sacramento legislators assembled amid stands of hot video lights to celebrate 150 years of California legislative history, joking their way through a raucous session that occasionally echoed political issues that plagued the 1853 California capital's original session.*[160]

# An Outline of the History
## of the Benicia Capitol Building

| Year | Date | Location | Occurrence |
|---|---|---|---|
| 1807 | July 4 | Monterey | General Vallejo born |
| 1846 | | Benicia | Lieutenant William T. Sherman and Lieutenant James Hardie select Benicia as site of "Military Reservation" |
| 1847 | | Benicia | Cavalry and infantry occupy Benicia point |
| 1849 | April 30 | Benicia | "Post at point near Benicia" founded |
| | September–October | Monterrey | California constitutional convention |
| | December 20 | San Jose | First legislature meets |
| 1850 | September 9 | | Statehood |
| 1851 | December 30 | San Jose | Last day of legislature in San Jose |
| | December 30 | San Francisco | One-day meeting of the legislature |
| 1852 | January 5 | Vallejo | Third session of legislature |
| | January 12 | Vallejo | The legislature leaves |

| Year | Date | Location | Occurrence |
|------|------|----------|------------|
| 1852 | January 16 | Sacramento | Temporary capital in Sacramento |
| | May 4 | Sacramento | Legislature leaves |
| 1853 | January 3 | Vallejo | Legislature meets again in Vallejo |
| | February 4 | Vallejo | Legislature decamps for Benicia |
| | February 11 | Benicia | Legislature meets in Benicia |
| 1854 | February 25 | Benicia | Legislature leaves for Sacramento for good |

# Notes

## Chapter 1

1. James E. Lessenger, "Preaching Politics from the Pulpit: Rev. Sylvester Woodbridge and the Demise of the First Protestant Church in California," *Solano Historian* 29, no. 1–2 (March 2014): 16–31.

## Chapter 2

2. Alfred L. Kroeber, *The Patwin and Their Neighbors* (Berkeley: University of California Press, 1933).
3. Patti J. Johnson, *Handbook of North American Indians: California* (Washington, D.C.: Government Printing Office, 1978).
4. Paul C. Johnson et al, ed., *The California Missions: A Pictorial History* (Menlo Park, CA: Lane Book Company, 1964).
5. Robert S. Smilie, *The Sonoma Mission, San Francisco Solano de Sonoma: The Founding, Ruin and Restoration of California's 21st Mission* (Fresno, CA: Valley Publishers, 1975).
6. Charles Chapman, *A History of California: The Spanish Period* (New York: Macmillan Company, 1939).
7. W.W. Robinson, *Land in California: The Story of Mission Lands, Ranchos, Squatters, Mining Claims, Railroad Grants, Land Scrip, Homesteads* (Los Angeles: University of California Press, 1948).

8. Alan Rosenus, *General Vallejo and the Advent of the Americans* (Berkeley, CA: Heyday Books, 1995).

9. Ibid.

10. Ibid.

11. Ibid.

12. John Currey, "Judge Currey and Spanish Land Grants in Solano," *Solano Historian* (December 1990).

13. Ibid.

14. Robinson, *Land in California*.

15. Ibid.

16. Ibid.

17. James M. Ramirez, *The Legend of Francisco Solano* (Fairfield, CA: James Stevenson Publisher, 2006).

18. Zoe Green Radcliffe, "Robert Baylor Semple: Pioneer," *California Historical Society Quarterly* 6, no. 2 (June 1927): 130–58.

19. Woodrow J. Hanson, "Robert Semple: Pioneer, Promoter, Politician," *California Historical Society Quarterly* 41, no. 3 (September 1962): 223–35.

20. Agreement between Mariano Vallejo and Robert Semple, *Californian*, December 22, 1846.

21. Robert Bruegmann, *Benicia: Portrait of an Early California* (Fairfield, CA: James Stevenson Publisher, 1980).

22. Deed for Benicia City from M.G. Vallejo, to Semple and Larkin, the *Californian*. May 19, 1847. Agreement between Thomas O. Larkin and R. Semple, the *Californian*, May 19, 1847. The Deed for Benicia City from General Vallejo to Semple and Larkin was executed on May 19, 1847. The Semple deeds were recorded on December 10, 1847, and the Larkin deeds were recorded December 18, 1847. There were no deeds from Larkin to Semple after Larkin withdrew from the Benicia land project, and there was no land swap between Larkin and Semple for Larkin's Colusa properties. After Semple's death in 1854, the remaining Benicia properties that were in his name became the property of his wife, who in turn sold them.

23. Herbert H. Bancroft, "Local Annals of the North, 1846–1848" in *The Works of Hubert Howe Bancroft, Volume XXII* (San Francisco, CA: The History Company, 1886), 670–74.

24. Josephine W. Cowell, *History of Benicia Arsenal* (Berkeley, CA: Howell-North Press, 1963).

25. Ibid.

26. Title to the military reservation was recorded in phases:

Deed from Robert Semple and wife and others (Larkin), dated April 16, 1849, and recorded July 5, 1949, in book C, pages 295–96 of records by L.W. Boggs, *alcalde* for Sonoma. Also recorded in Benicia, November 19, 1849, in book A, pages 460–61 of the records of Solano County.

Deed of release from Mariano G. Vallejo dated December 27, 1854, not recorded.

Deed of release from Thomas O. Larkin, dated December 30, 1854, and recorded January 24, 1855, in book I, page 347 of the deed records of Solano County.

Deed of release from Bethnel Phelps, dated January 20, 1855, and recorded January 20, 1855 in book H, pages 340–41 of the records of Solano County.

27. Thomas Lucy, "General John Frisbie, Solano Entrepreneur," *Solano Historian* (December 1985).

28. Thomas Lucy, "Town Site of Vallejo and the Suscol Controversy," *Solano Historian* (December 1988).

29. Documents Pertaining to the Adjudication of Private Land Claims in California, 318ND (circa 1852–92); Bancroft Library, University of California, BANC MSS Land Case files (1852–92); BANC MSS C-A 300 film.

30. Letter from the secretary of the interior, Columbus Delano, in answer to a resolution of the House of June 8 last, relative to the status of military reservation no. 7, opposite Mare Island, California. Washington, D.C.: House of Representatives, (1872).

31. A.T Britton, in the United States land office for the district of lands subject to sale at San Francisco. Bancroft Library, University of California; Documents Pertaining to the Adjudication; BANC MSS C-A 300 FILM.

32. United States v. Vallejo, 66 U.S.541 (1861).

33. Ibid.

34. Ibid.

35. Paul W. Gates, "The Suscol Principle, Preemption, and California Latifundia," *Pacific Historical Review* 39, no. 4 (November 1970), 453–71.

36. Abraham Lincoln, letter to Hon. Caleb B. Smith, Secretary of the Interior (October 7, 1862).

37. M. Potter, *Rancho Suscol Report No. 20* (Washington, D.C.: Thirty-Seventh Congress, 1863).

38. "The Suscol Grant," *California Farmer and Journal of Useful Sciences* (May 22, 1863).

39. James Speed, *Opinion of the Attorney General in the Case of Soscol* (sic) *Rancho* (Washington, D.C.: Attorney General's Office: May 26, 1866).

40. City of Benicia Board of Trustees, *Official Documents in Relation to Land Titles in the City of Benicia* (Benicia, CA: City of Benicia, 1867).

## Chapter 3

41. Lessenger, "Preaching Politics," 16–31.

42. David D. Clinton, "The Decline of the Southern Chivalry in California: The 1860 Presidential Election" (master's thesis, Sacramento State University, 1975).

43. Kevin Starr, *California: A History* (New York: Modern Library, 2005).

44. John C. Davenport, *The US-Mexico Border: The Treaty of Guadalupe Hidalgo* (Philadelphia, PA: Chelsea House Publishers, 2005), 48.

45. Richard Horsman, "The Northwest Ordinance and the Shaping of an Expanding Republic," *Wisconsin Magazine of History* (1989): 21–32.

46. Woodrow J. Hansen, "Robert Semple: Pioneer, Promoter, Politician," *California Historical Quarterly* 41, no. 3 (September 1962): 223–35.

47. Zoe Green Radcliff, "Robert Baylor Semple, Pioneer," *California Historical Society Quarterly* 6, no. 2 (June 1927): 130–58.

48. Mary Grace Kos, "California's Search for a Capital Site, 1846–1879" (doctoral degree thesis, Graduate School of Saint Louis University, 1962), 81.

49. Walter Colton, *Three Years in California* (New York: A.S. Barnes and Company, 1850).

50. Kos, "California's Search," 92.

## Chapter 4

51. Kos, "California's Search," 94.

52. Ibid. 97.

53. Ibid. 100.

54. Ibid. 108.

55. Ibid. 114.

56. Ibid. 119.

57. Ibid. 124.

58. *Alta California*, May 9, 1850, 2.

59. Herbert E. Bolton, "The Admission of California," *University of California Chronicle* 20, no. 4 (October 1913): 565–66.
60. Journal of the Senate, State of California (1851), 560.
61. Kos, "California's Search," 135.
62. Ibid. 141.
63. Ibid. 143.
64. *Alta California*, May 27, 1851.
65. Kos, "California's Search," 145.
66. Report of James S. Graham in reference to Building at Vallejo, December 25, 1851, Messages and Reports to the Governor, Drawer 12, Secretary of State Records Group, California State Archives.
67. Kos, "California's Search," 147.

## Chapter 5

68. Ibid. 148.
69. Ibid. 149.
70. Ibid. 159.
71. Ibid. 168.
72. Ibid. 172.
73. Ibid. 173.
74. *Daily Alta California*, May 12, 1852.
75. Kos, "California's Search," 175.
76. *Sacramento Daily Union*, January 2, 1852.
77. Kos, "California's Search," 178.
78. Ibid. 191.
79. Ibid. 193.

## Chapter 6

80. Benicia City Council minutes, May 7, 1850.
81. *Daily Alta California*, July 15, 1851.
82. Benicia City Council minutes, June 8, 1850.
83. Ibid. May 17, 1851.
84. Ibid. February 9, 1852.
85. Ibid. February 19, 1852.
86. Ibid. March 19, 1852.

87. Ibid. June 7 to August 9, 1852.

88. Ibid. August 25, 1852.

89. Ibid. August 30, 1852,

90. Ibid. October 4, 1852.

91. State Department of Public Works, *Restoration of the Benicia State Capitol* (Benicia, CA: Sacramento Division of Architecture, 1958).

92. *California Daily Alta*, December 15, 1852.

93. Benicia City Council minutes, January 3, 1852.

94. Ibid. February 21, 1852.

## *Chapter 7*

95. *Daily Alta*, February 10, 1853.

96. *Sacramento Daily Union*, January 3, 1854.

97. State of California, *Journal of the Fourth Assembly* (San Francisco: George Kerr State Printer, 1853).

98. Ibid.

99. Rudolph M. Lapp, *Afro-Americans in California* (San Francisco, CA: Boyd and Fraser Publishing Company, 1987).

100. State of California, State Constitution (Monterey, CA: State Printer, 1849).

101. The Statutes of California passed at the third session of the legislature (San Francisco: George Kerr State Printer, 1852).

102. Rudolph M. Lapp, *Blacks in Gold Rush California* (New Haven, CT: Yale University Press, 1977).

103. State of California, Laws of the State of California (Benicia, CA: George Kerr State Printer, 1854).

104. *Sacramento Daily Alta*, February 8, 1854.

105. Henry S. Clubs, *The Maine Liquor Law: Its Origin, History and Results* (New York: Fowler and Wells, 1856).

106. "The Governor's Message," *Los Angeles Star*, January 21, 1854.

107. Charles J McClain, "The Chinese Struggle for Civil Rights in Nineteenth Century America: The First Phase, 1850–1870," *California Law Review* 72 (1984): 529.

108. "California Legislature, Fifth Session," *Sacramento Daily Union*, January 20, 1854.

109. "Testimony in the Alleged Bribery Case," *Daily Alta California*, January 29, 1854.

110. "Legislative Correspondence," *Sacramento Daily Union*, January 31, 1854.

## Chapter 8

111. Journal of the Fifth Session of the Legislature of the State of California, (Sacramento: B.B. Redding State Printer, 1854).
112. *Sacramento Daily Union*, January 25, 1854.
113. *Sacramento Daily Union*, October 20, 1853.
114. *Benicia Vendette*, December 31, 1853.
115. *Sacramento Daily Union*, January 17, 1854.
116. *Sacramento Daily Union*, February 12, 1854.
117. *Sacramento Daily Union*, February 3, 1854.
118. Journal, January 13, 1854.
119. Kos, "California's Search," 177.
120. *Benicia Vedette*, December 23, 1854.
121. Journal, February 24,1854.
122. Journal, February 28, 1854.
123. Kos, "California's Search," 225.
124. Ibid. 229.
125. *Daily Alta California*, September 29, 1854, 2.
126. Kos, "California's Search," 234.
127. *Sacramento Daily Union*, November 3, 1854.
128. *Sacramento Daily Union*, February 3, 1855.

## Chapter 9

129. Benicia City Council Minutes, May 30, 1854.
130. Ibid. September 11, 1854.
131. Ibid. November 20, 1854.
132. Ibid. November 24, 1854.
133. Ibid. February 12, 1855.
134. Ibid. July 2, 1855.
135. Ibid. October 18, 1855.
136. Ibid. November 12, 1855.
137. Ibid. October 1, 1856.
138. Ibid. April 5, 1858.
139. Ibid. December 29, 1859.
140. Ibid. August 4, 1862.

## Chapter 10

141. Julia Businger and Beverly Phelan, Images of America: *Benicia* (Charleston, SC: Arcadia Publishing, 2004).
142. Josephine Cowell, *History of Benicia Arsenal, Benicia, California* (San Francisco: Howell-North Books, 1963).
143. Steven DeBenedetti, Statement of March 14, 195, Benicia Historical Museum, DeBenedetti files.
144. "Capitol Building Restoration Underway," *Benicia Herald*, May 3, 1956.
145. Steven DeBenedetti's scrapbook, Benicia Historical Museum, DeBenedetti files.
146. "City Hall Unsafe," *Vallejo Times-Herald*, April 8, 1955.
147. "Rites Held for Benicia's New Library," *Vallejo Times-Herald*, May 21, 1956.
148. "Rededication of City Hall," *Vallejo Times-Herald*, November 4, 1986.

## Chapter 11

149. "City Council Moves," *Benicia Times-Herald*, March 3, 1956.
150. Minutes of Restoration Program Safety Meeting, October 1956.
151. Minard Lafever, *The Modern Builder's Guide* (New York: Paine and Burgess, 1846).
152. "Detailed Care Shows in Capitol Rebuilding," *Vallejo Times-Herald*, March 10, 1958.
153. "Original Capitol Lock Discovered," *Visalia Times-Herald*, January 2, 1956.
154. "Restoration Job Begun by State," *Vallejo News-Chronicle*, May 3, 1956.
155. "Old Capitol Gets All Furnishings," *Vallejo Times-Herald*, February 28, 1958.

## Chapter 12

156. "Benicia State Capitol Dedication Fulfillment of Native Son's Dream," *Benician*, March 4, 1958.

157. "Luncheon in Honor of the Dedication of the Benicia State Capitol Building," program, Native Sons of the Golden West, March 15, 1958.

158. "Earthquake," *Visalia Times-Herald*, February 29, 1960.

159. Rich Cartiere, "Benicia Fights to Get Capital Back," *Vacaville Reporter*, October 9, 1983.

160. Richard Toronto, "They Came Back to Visit," *Benicia Herald*, May 21, 1993.

# Index

# About the Author

Jim Lessenger is a physician by profession and a historian by hobby. While he has published thirty-one professional articles and two books in the field of medicine, this is his fourth publication in the field of history. Since the fourth grade, Jim has been fascinated by California history. He roamed the state looking at places of historical interest to write about, until he found Benicia, which is loaded with enough history and stories to fill a shelf of books. He is an active volunteer at the Benicia History Museum, where he researches subjects and participates in the building and installation of exhibits. Dr. Lessenger still practices medicine by volunteering as the medical director of a free clinic and drug treatment community.

*Visit us at*
www.historypress.com
..................................................................